THE LTL CARRIER'S PROFITABILITY BLUEPRINT

BY

ROBERT L SULLIVAN III

THE LTL CARRIER'S PROFITABILITY BLUEPRINT

ISBN: 978-1-647043-54-4

This book is printed on acid-free paper.

Printed in the United States of America

Dedication

This book is dedicated to my beautiful sweetheart and loving wife Eileen. Sweetheart, thank you for putting up with "Mr. High Maintenance"! You truly are my inspiration and motivation. Thank you for being my travel buddy and letting me drag you all over the country when I truly know there are many times you just really wanted to stay home. I promise I will slow down a little…in about 10 years! Love Ya!!

As I did with my first book, I would also like to dedicate this book to Bruce H. Griffin Sr. and Bruce H. Griffin Jr. Thank you for being so generous and helping me get my business started. I could never repay the goodness and kindness you have shown me. You both taught me a lot about life and business. Thank You!

ACKNOWLEDGEMENTS

I would like to say thank you to all my current and former clients for allowing me to become a part of your life, your company, and your family. We learned a lot together getting our nose bloodied in the trenches. We had laughs, concerns, rough patches, anxious moments, but we never gave up! I am so grateful for each of you!

PREFACE

As I was writing this book, memories of my journey in the LTL industry began flooding my mind. I paused for a few minutes, and after reflecting realized how blessed I am to have had the opportunity to work with so many wonderful, giving, intelligent, courageous, and passionate leaders through the years. I have learned so much from every company that purchased my system and installed my methodology. To all of you, thank you!

My journey in LTL began when I was in high school, but I had always been fascinated by tractor-trailers. I remembering going to Ford, GMC, and Chevrolet dealers and grabbing their brochures on the trucks and tractors they manufactured, reading through them with a passion. I could stand in my front yard and listen to a truck coming down the highway and without seeing it tell you what make of truck it was.

When I was in high school I made certain I got to know the local pickup and delivery drivers that ran their peddle route in my town, Myrtle Beach. I knew the Overnite Transportation driver, the Standard Trucking Company driver, and the Southeastern Freight Lines driver. After school I would go look for them just to say hello.

One day I was talking to the Overnite driver and he asked me if I would like to ride with him and help him deliver his freight. *Are you kidding? Wow,* I thought. At the end of the day he actually paid me with petty cash for helping him. I couldn't believe it! I got to ride in a tractor-trailer all day and I even got paid! Life was good. That began my career in the LTL industry.

Many people, including most of you reading this book, probably do not remember the days of regulation and the ICC (interstate Commerce Commission). I would like to share an interesting story from that time that we would never see today in this deregulated, highly competitive industry.

In the summer, E.C. Bailey, the Overnite driver, would pick me up at a gas station when he arrived at the beach, which was usually around 10:30 or 11 a.m. His terminal was in Florence, South Carolina, about 60 or 70 miles from Myrtle Beach. Back then freight on pallets or skids was basically non-existent; almost everything was touched by hand. I remember our first stop was a wholesale company where we would deliver cartons of cigarettes. I would open the door on the trailer carefully because the trailer was so packed; often cases of cigarettes fell on me. The 45-foot trailer was packed from front to rear, floor to ceiling. A typical day would be 20 to 25 stops and we would normally finish around 6 or 6:30 p.m.

It was fascinating how all the drivers worked together. They had become friends through the years of running the same route. Around noon we would all meet at the Walgreens drugstore for lunch at the small counter in the rear of the store. We would have a quick lunch and after head to the Pavilion parking lot ,where the drivers would back their trailers up to one another to divide up the freight based on where it was headed along the Grand Strand, which ran from Little River, South Carolina in the north down to Pawley's Island in the south.

One driver would handle Myrtle Beach proper and Ocean Boulevard, another Myrtle Beach Air Force Base (now the commercial airport for Myrtle Beach) to Pawley's Island, another would handle the north end of Myrtle Beach, and another would take Windy Hill Beach up to Little River. Even though Overnite paid me out of petty cash, I rode with the driver that wound up with the most stops. One day I might be with the Southeastern driver and the next with the Standard Trucking driver. While the driver was getting the bill signed I would move the next stop's freight to the rear of the trailer. We were a lean, mean productive machine!

At the end of the day we would all meet back at the Pavilion parking lot and straighten out the bills, any returned or refused shipments, and money collected. It was not uncommon to see a Southeastern driver delivering an Overnite Transportation driver's bill and freight.

You would never see that in today's environment. Years later, when I was a manager of a Southeastern terminal, the Overnite manager would call and ask to borrow a tractor or a trailer for the day and I asked the same of him from time to time. Imagine that happening today! It was a different time.

Ironically, little did I know that years later, after getting out of the military, I would be peddling freight myself for Southeastern Freight Lines and my route would be Myrtle Beach out of the Florence terminal! Isn't life absolutely amazing? I drove a U-model Mack with a duplex transmission. We used to joke that our tractor had a 2/60 air conditioner, which, for you young whippersnappers, is two windows down at 60 mph. Occasionally I would get to drive a White 9000 with a Detroit engine and 10-speed RoadRanger transmission. Loved the sound of that engine. I remember taking my road test in a cabover gasoline-powered International tractor hooked to a 40,000-pound load of food products going to W Lee Flowers, a grocery warehouse distributor in, I believe, Lake City or Scranton, South Carolina.

As you can see, I have spent a lifetime in the LTL industry. I still say the best job in the industry is local P&D driver. But enough of memory lane.

Those were the simple days. As we all know, it is getting tougher and tougher to make money in this industry. With all the crazy things carriers and customers are doing, it is absolutely critical that a carrier not only knows, but also understands costs and how they behave with a change in volume or activity and a change in capacity and capacity utilization.

We all experience moments that are life changing. The first time it happened to me was in Vietnam. The birth of my two sons was next. From a career standpoint, my life-changing moment occurred in 1977. I was managing a terminal in Augusta, Georgia and I came to work one morning to hear that my largest account had filed for Chapter 11. The company was a huge organization! As I tried to understand the event, I told myself that there had to be some warning signs or signals that alerted management that they were in trouble. I just did not understand how a company that size could cease to exist.

About two weeks later, I picked up a Business Week magazine and read an article about a turnaround manager who went into a furniture manufacturing company that was failing and turned them around to strong profitability. I was hooked! I remember saying to myself, *Wow! That's exciting!* So I have spent my adult life looking for case studies of both successful companies and failed companies, researching to learn why some declined and failed. I came to understand that you don't study failure to avoid failure, you study failure to succeed!

Through the years my passion for what I do has never subsided. I am just as hungry and passionate today as I was back in 1977. As you will read many times in this book, a leader must make the personal commitment to continue to learn and grow to continue to achieve at higher levels. The operating environment is always moving to higher and higher levels and becomes more complex each day. You have to keep up or your value to your organization will diminish.

The one common denominator I have found in all the companies that I have worked with that were stagnant or in a state of decline is this: They did not understand their costs. These carriers tried to run their business from an income statement. Two problems with that: first, you're always reacting to it because the events that created that statement happened six weeks earlier or more, and second, the statement was in the traditional EBITDA format. That format prevents management from "seeing" their problems because they have fixed and variable costs mixed together. Running your business from an income statement is like driving a car forward by looking in the rearview mirror.

Something else that drove decline was when the carriers used traditional, old-fashioned productivity measurements from the era of regulation, such as stops per hour, bills per hour, and pounds per man-hour. Those measurements perpetuate inefficiencies because they are "in the mix," too macro, and cannot measure capacity. A carrier's productivity level drives the income statement.

Finally, the failing or stagnant carriers used traditional "cost-based" or "activity-based" costing systems. The major problem with these systems is they cannot measure capacity or capacity utilization. They assume the carrier is operating at 100% capacity and that is simply not true. When using those traditional systems, the carrier is trying to pass on the cost of their inefficiencies and unused capacity to the customer in the form of price. A carrier's inefficiencies and excess capacity belong to the carrier, not the customer. Also, because those systems cannot measure capacity or capacity utilization, they cannot factor in the value of unused capacity to the carrier in the costing and pricing process. The carrier leaves market share they should be handling in the marketplace because they cost themselves out of business. An LTL carrier is a highly capital-intense business, and the intensity is driven by the capacity provided to the marketplace. If you cannot measure your capacity in operations and the percent of utilization, you truly do not know your costs.

This industry has very competent leaders. I know because I have worked with hundreds over the years. When carriers fail to succeed, the problem is not leadership, but that the costing systems and measurements leaders use prevent them from truly understanding their costs and their company. Remedying this situation is the purpose of this book.

A company is made up of hundreds and sometimes thousands of employees, and they depend on the leaders of the company to be competent and capable so they can provide and improve the quality of life for their loved ones. To the best of my ability, I wanted, in writing this book, to provide the leaders of an LTL carrier with a blueprint that could be used to make the leader stronger and the company stronger; I wanted to take what I have learned through the years and give it back to you, the reader.

To the extent I have done that, I am humbled. I have tried so hard to get it right in this book because I want leaders and companies to succeed. That is my passion and purpose in life! If I fall short in that purpose, I apologize.

I believe writing a book is the most difficult thing I have ever done professionally, so this is my second book and my last. I hope it will serve you well!

To all of you reading this book who have let me become a part of your company through the years: Thank you and God bless!

TABLE OF CONTENTS

Chapter 1   Putting Decline and Failure in Perspective 1

Chapter 2   Understanding the Game 16

Chapter 3   The Barrier of Complexity 35

Chapter 4   Pickup and Delivery Capacity Management 48

Chapter 5   Dock and Linehaul Trailer Utilization..................................59

Chapter 6   Customer Base Analysis...69

Chapter 7   Performance Based Incentive Compensation 79

Chapter 8   Developing and Implementing a Strategy 94

Chapter 9   Turning Strategy into Action...105

Chapter 10   The Blueprint: Bringing it all Together..............................117

Summary..132

CHAPTER 1

Putting Decline and Failure in Perspective

When the group or civilization declines, it is through no mystic limitation of a corporate life, but through the failure of its political or intellectual leaders to meet the challenge of change.

—**Will and Ariel Durant,** *The Lessons of History*

Leadership: Understanding the Game

You may be wondering why the first chapter in this book focuses on decline and failure, given that you are reading *The LTL Carrier's Profitability Blueprint*. It is just as important to understand why some LTL carriers fail as it is to understand why some LTL carriers prosper and grow. Understanding decline and success is the beginning of your personal journey to becoming a student of this ever-changing industry, so you can continue to learn and grow, which will lead to achievement at an extremely high level. The intent of this chapter is to put you on that path to success.

As a college football coach, I learned firsthand the importance of adaptability in preventing organizational decline. With each new season, the game changed and became more complex; the coaches got smarter, and the players bigger, stronger, and faster. I realized that I had to become a student of the game or I would be left behind, and my value to the team, coaching staff, and school would diminish. I had to make the personal commitment to continue to learn and grow so I could continue to achieve at higher and higher levels as the game changed.

Business leaders must make the same kind of commitment to growth and adaptability. Since the game is always changing, leaders who do not prioritize learning and growth will plateau, and their businesses' risk for decline will increase. You have to lay the praise for a company's success or the blame for its failure on the president's desk. As the old saying goes, the buck stops there.

It can be easy to lose perspective when we stay so busy and face so many distractions throughout the workday. If someone falls down, we look at that person and say, "Don't just lie there doing nothing—do pushups!"

When I started my business in 1986, the industry was still trying to understand the impact of deregulation (and even today that is still the case for many carriers). If you have been in the industry as long as I have, you know that hundreds of carriers failed within the first 10 years of deregulation. Many carriers that failed were icons of the industry, but they were too slow to change, refused to change, or were unable to change.

A company has three resources at hand that can help it respond to change: human, physical, and financial. That's it. Over the course of my career, I have worked with carriers of all sizes, and I have determined that the quality of human resources determines the level of financial resources, which in turn determines the quality and level of physical resources. It's all about leadership—that's all you've got! It's not just leadership at the top, though; a successful business has quality leadership all the way down to the dock supervisor and dispatcher levels.

Decline and Failure:
Are External Forces or Internal Forces Responsible?

Decline and failure, from an economic standpoint, means a situation in which a company's return on invested capital is less than the rates on similar investments, and the decline on return is gaining momentum. Understood this way, a company can be an economic failure long before it becomes a failure the legal sense because it continues to be able to meet its current financial obligations.

A carrier's health falls into one of three stages: trauma, stabilization, and back-to-growth. It is critical that leaders of a carrier in the trauma stage understand it cannot jump to a strategy that is meant for carriers in the growth stage. Because carriers have a tendency to overestimate revenues and underestimate costs, a carrier in the trauma stage will simply run out of cash if it adopts a strategy meant for the growth stage.

A carrier in the trauma stage is experiencing deep losses, cash shortfalls, and a waterlogged balance sheet. At this point the bankers are having the meetings in their office, rather than yours. If the owners have assets or equity they are being asked—no, told—to guarantee them at this point to even think about bridge financing, in most cases. It is not a very comfortable position to be in.

The carrier must focus on a strategy and tactics that will move it from the trauma stage to the stabilization stage. Once the carrier is stable, which usually means a year or three consecutive quarters of profitability after leaving the trauma stage, the carrier can develop a modest growth strategy and tactics that will move it forward. Unless the carrier has extremely deep pockets, jumping stages financially will not work. The carrier must progress sequentially from the trauma stage to the stabilization stage and then to the growth stage.

In most cases, the carrier has entered the trauma stage because current leadership didn't see it coming. This means that the current leadership's thinking and actions will not be able to move the company forward without some sort of outside help.

I often hear leaders blame the economy, or competition, or pricing, or, or, or. . . External forces outside the company always get the blame, but both internal forces and external forces always create challenges for leadership. Unless a company has one source of revenue—examples might include a single-source defense contractor tied to the government, or a company that supplies products only to one manufacturer, like automobile industry—external forces alone cannot be blamed for decline and failure.

It is tough to build high market share or to hang onto high market share and continually improve long-term profitability in the face of intense competition. As harsh as this may sound, some companies have no reason to exist. These are companies that have no customer base of their own. They haven't grown in years and cash and financial resources are always scarce. In many markets, there is room for only two or three carriers at the market leader level. Any carrier below that market-leader level barely gets by in good times and becomes extremely vulnerable in bad times. Carriers at this lower level fight among each other for the business the market leaders either don't want, can't service, or can't make money on. That, my friends, is a very uncomfortable and risky position to be in.

I have found that a change in external forces on a company brings the company's internal weaknesses to the surface, weaknesses such as ineffective leadership; outdated systems or methodologies; and lack of vision, strategy, and tactics. The slide into decline begins with these internal weaknesses. I read an analogy somewhere that sums up this situation quite well: "Blaming external forces for the failure of a company is like the captain of an overloaded ship caught in a storm blaming a 2-foot wave for its sinking. Yes, the 2-foot wave sank the overloaded ship, but what about all the other ships still afloat nearby whose captains checked and heeded the weather forecast and prepared for the storm?"

It's all about leadership. I learned as a coach that you couldn't take a two-star athlete and turn that athlete into a five-star athlete (the percentages are against you on accomplishing such a feat). That is why all the schools fight for the four- and five-star athletes. Coaches understand the importance of having blue-chip players. Remember that the quality of a carrier's human resources determines the level of financial resources the carrier has to work with, which in turn determines the quality and level of physical resources the carrier has. Leadership determines success.

Bottom line: Decline and failure occurs at a managerial level. A company is a managerial failure long before it becomes an economic or legal failure, so management must be aware of the company's health and be on the lookout for signs of decline.

How Should the Management Team Watch for Decline?

Stagnant or Declining Sales: Running a business is like riding a bicycle: You're either moving forward or you're falling over. I tell all my clients that first and foremost, companies should consider themselves to be a sales and marketing organization. It doesn't matter if you are a department store, hardware store, car dealership, ice cream parlor, or trucking company: You have to be a sales and marketing organization that just happens to make money by selling clothes, hardware, cars, or ice cream, or by hauling freight.

Variable Cost as a Percent of Sales: If an LTL carrier's sales are stagnant or declining, the next number management had better check is variable cost as a percent of sales. Chances are that if the company is experiencing flat or declining sales, variable cost as a percent of sales is rising. If that is the case, contribution dollars to cover fixed costs and overhead is declining, and the breakeven point is deteriorating. A 1% increase in variable cost will increase the breakeven point 3% to 5% or more—not what you want to see! The key relationship for an LTL carrier is variable cost as a percent of revenue. There is an entire chapter later in the book devoted to that relationship.

I have found that if variable cost as a percent of revenue exceeds 70%, the carrier is losing money. The carrier could be at breakeven at 70–71%, but above that number, the carrier is in a loss position. Another important figure is the relationship between revenue and shipment growth. If the percent of shipment growth is at a higher rate than revenue growth, the carrier is losing money.

Revenue, Variable Cost, and Contribution Dollars Per Shipment: This is a very important relationship to understand and watch. If the relationship of variable cost per shipment and revenue per shipment is not improving, that means the ratio of contribution dollars per shipment is declining. Above we talked about the importance of sales growth; if shipment count is stagnant or declining and contribution dollars per shipment is declining, the situation is getting uglier. There is a delicate balance between quality and quantity of revenue that is critical to the profitability of the company. An LTL carrier is a *very* capital-intense company and the level of variable cost drives that capital intensity.

<u>A Brief Plateau Is Acceptable, but Not a Long Plateau:</u> When a company hits a sales or profitability plateau, it is acceptable to pause for a short time to recover its direction and bearings. However, an extended plateau puts the company at risk. What do I consider a short period of time? No longer than 9 months to a year. It really depends on the severity of the situation, and each carrier is different. Remember the bicycle analogy? When a company plateaus it has three options. It can do nothing (and wait for a business hazard to come along like that 2-foot wave and sink it), it can implement stringent profit improvement programs, or it can sell off losing assets and regroup. One thing is certain: if the company does not choose at least one of the latter two options, it will fail.

Implementing strong profit improvement programs means a change in the culture of the company, which is a very difficult process to get through. We will discuss it at great length in the chapter "The Barrier of Complexity," which was actually a chapter in my first book, *The Formula: Building Competitive Advantage*. Through the years so many leaders have told me that the chapter was their "aha" moment that I have decided it was important to include an updated version in this book. Whether or not a carrier breaks through the barrier of complexity determines whether a carrier will survive and grow or fail.

The second option, selling off or closing losing assets, rarely happens. I have been in business for many years and I have heard owner after owner tell me they would rather grow at 3% and have a profit margin of 10% than grow at 15% and have a profit margin of 6%. But the funny thing is that I have never met an owner who will actually do that. Shrinking the size of the company is extremely emotional.

The action a company takes depends on the severity of the situation. One thing is absolutely certain, though, based on my experience: if a company that has plateaued does not grow and implement strong profit improvement initiatives, it will enter the decline phase.

In many cases a company will try to throw itself off this plateau with some growth-for-growth's-sake strategy and eat up the last of its available credit. Usually when the carrier is at this point they are so leveraged and cash is so short that any project large enough to boost them off the plateau and move forward is too large to accomplish given the human and financial resources at hand. These initiatives also fail because, as stated earlier, the company will overestimate revenues and underestimate costs.

When I have agreed to help carriers that are stagnant or declining I find—without exception—that they are treating the symptoms instead of larger underlying problems. I have found that it's not that the leaders cannot solve their problems, but that they cannot see their problems. Often they cannot see their problems because they are using outdated costing and productivity systems and measurements that extend back to the days of regulation, and cost models not designed for our industry, but "modified" for the industry. Remember, the game is always changing and moving to a higher level. When a carrier does not change with the environment, complexity within the organization increases. Increasing complexity is competitive disadvantage because it creates what I call "management by thrashabout." The answer to complexity is simplicity. Eliminating management by thrashabout and creating simplicity is the purpose of this book.

The Three Stages in the Business Life Cycle: The View from 40,000 Feet

A carrier can find itself in one of three stages or moving between two stages. The three basic stages, as noted earlier in this chapter, are trauma, stabilization, and back-to-growth. I use the term "back to growth" and not just "growth" because every carrier, at one time or another, finds itself in either the trauma stage or the stabilization stage. It is important to recognize each stage because a carrier in the trauma stage cannot adopt the strategy or tactics of the back-to-growth stage. In doing so, the carrier might find a little short-term success, but invariably the carrier will find itself back in the trauma stage. Just as a patient brought to the emergency room with life-threatening trauma must go through the process of stabilization and then back to growth from a medical standpoint, so must a company in the trauma stage.

Though a book could be devoted to each of the three stages, we will look at each stage from the 40,000-feet perspective to give the reader a basic understanding of what each stage looks like. The purpose of examining each stage is to give readers the ability to place their organization in one of the three stages.

The Trauma Stage

A carrier in the trauma stage can be mildly traumatic or severely threatened, depending on the cash flow position and the strength of the balance sheet. Unfortunately, in the majority of cases the balance sheet is usually waterlogged if a carrier is in this stage. The next area to evaluate is whether the solution called for is an operating fix or a sales fix. If there is enough volume to work with, cost cutting can be implemented, which makes this a pretty quick fix. If the volume of business is not available, however, it's going to be a long journey and take a lot of cash to set things right. This is why I encourage all my clients to adopt the strategy of thinking like a sales and marketing organization; a sales fix takes a long time and burns up a lot of cash! As we say in the South, high water covers a lot of stumps.

Getting an LTL carrier out of the Trauma stage is much more difficult than bringing a manufacturing company out of the same kind of situation, especially if the solution is a sales fix. A carrier has to balance service with cash needs. A carrier that needs a sales fix must improve sales volume while continuing to serve the customer and providing competitive service, or it will lose market share to the competition and become unable to grow the company

The basic business thrust in the trauma stage is to manage for immediate cash. I am sure you have heard the old saying that cash is king!

Accounts receivable is area I find in terrible shape at many companies. Not only do I find a great deal of cash outstanding at 60 days or more, but in many cases I also find that there is no system in place to work AR on a daily basis. I recently worked with a client to turn around a carrier. Soon after our work together ended, I got a call from the owner. He did not understand why his carrier was profitable, but he still needed to continue putting cash into the company. The reason was very simple. They had allowed their AR to become waterlogged because they had discontinued working on the process we put in place.

Another area to watch is the shop. If your company performs its own maintenance on equipment, and particularly if your company has shops at multiple terminals, you need to jump into this. In many cases I have found inventories that would give you nightmares. Also keep an eye on purchasing habits and vendors. The maintenance department has a tendency to be disconnected from the rest of the company and surprisingly, in many cases, has no idea of the company's financial position.

Simply tightening up controls in every department will improve working capital for the company.

The customer base is an area that is sacred, but it too must be part of the process. This is a *very* tricky issue and I recommend exercising extreme caution because as I have noted, most carriers think they know their costs, but they really do not. If you are using operating ratio as your basis of customer profitability, you really do not know a customer's value to your company. I have seen companies that use operating ratio as the basis for customer profitability find themselves in the twilight zone in their retention and divestment decisions. A customer can have an operating ratio of 106, yet still be generating contribution dollars for the company. If you remove that customer, cash will worsen. Even using the traditional contribution margin approach from direct cost is inaccurate. Direct cost, from an accounting standpoint, has some fixed cost included. As a carrier you only want to remove those customers that are not covering their variable cost.

Let me give you an example. Customer A has an operating ratio of 106. The contribution method identifies the contribution dollars remaining to cover fixed cost and overheard after covering variable costs. Now, the definition of variable cost is costs that will change given a change in output or volume. Fixed costs do not change with a change in output or volume, within a relevant range. Customer A has an operating ratio of 106, but it is contributing 31% above the variable cost level to cover fixed cost and overhead. If the carrier removes this customer, the carrier not only must reduce the variable or direct cost, but also must reduce enough cost to cover the contribution dollars that were being generated by the customer, which they will now lose. Not understanding this principle will make the trauma stage even worse and the carrier may not understand why! When you start making changes to your customer base, you'd better know what the heck you're doing. Taking revenue out of the company is a dangerous game.

As for market share, the focus should not be on growth for growth's sake. The carrier must have a very accurate view of their customer base. A carrier in the trauma stage should raise prices and set a higher standard with regard to which new business they bring onboard. However, in most cases, just the opposite occurs. Many carriers fall into a growth-for-growth's sake mode, which is the beginning of the end. Underpricing is a perennial problem for carriers that decline. It is not the pricing department that is at fault, but the methodology used within the company to determine pricing. I truly believe, given market changes and rates over the last few years, that using operating ratio to determine pricing is dead. As an industry we just need to put it out of its misery.

The operations side of the business is where a catch-22 comes in. In the trauma stage, a carrier does everything within its power to reduce costs. This includes manpower reductions across the board, even though no one wants to put any person out of work. The balance for operations is between reducing costs and continuing to provide a level of service to customers that prevents them from jumping ship. Unfortunately, carriers using traditional measurements such as stops per hour, wages as a percent of revenue, pounds per man hour, and so on get it wrong. The job of the operations department is to control capacity. If you do not know your capacity and capacity utilization, which is impossible to do effectively without driving customers you want to keep away. Again, the problem here is not leadership, but instead inadequate, outdated measurements systems, which we will cover in greater depth in a later chapter.

The accounting side of the business needs to provide more managerial accounting reports rather than the traditional reports required by external forces. I am not suggesting that carriers dispense with that format; I am simply saying an internal variable or fixed income statement should be developed. Also, an operating profit and loss statement for each terminal location should be implemented. On the terminal level, leave out the fixed and semi-fixed cost and overhead. In most cases the terminal manager does not decide the rent on the terminal, the equipment the company purchases, the capital investments, or salary levels. What they do have control over is the variable cost of the terminal, such as P&D cost, dock cost, linehaul trailer utilization, and clerical cost. Terminal managers should be held accountable for those things they have control over. Simply put, the job of a terminal manager is to control variable costs and productivity and grow the revenue base by motivating the sales staff to give the pricing department opportunities for new business growth. The accounting thrust in this stage is to manage for cash, even at the expense of the P&L statement.

The Stabilization Stage

The carrier's objective in the trauma stage is simply to avoid failing and to bring cash to a positive position consistently. Once that occurs, the company can begin moving toward the stabilization stage. The basic objective for the stabilization stage is to maintain a conservative position. The company should focus on consistently operating above the breakeven point. This is all about proving to yourself and to your lenders that you have control over the business.

From a growth standpoint, the company could be flat. In this stage, in terms of importance, profit improvement is the thrust, cash flow is second in importance, and revenue growth brings up the rear.

1. Operations efficiencies are a main focus. This is the stage when the company must break through the barrier of complexity. Old operating paradigms and measurements must be replaced. If current leadership cannot change, the company must install leadership that will risk getting its nose bloodied by replacing old operating paradigms with new paradigms.

2. Control systems must improve and align. Most companies still operate in the old silo environment. Operations does their thing, sales does their thing, and costing and pricing does theirs. The silo model must be replaced with a system that will get these three areas on the same page, singing out of the same hymnal.

If the carrier cannot manage the quality and quantity of revenue and control variable cost, the back-to-growth stage will never reach its full potential. Those are fundamentals, and fundamentals are enduring.

A few years ago, I attended the annual convention of the American Football Coaches Association. An FBS (Football Bowl Subdivision) coach whose team had won a national championship a couple of years earlier spoke. To paraphrase his comments: a team can have the most complex offensive and defensive schemes, looks, and game plan. However, the team that wins the game on Saturday afternoon will most likely be the team that blocks the best and tackles the best.

In the same way, an LTL carrier that has the most efficient operation and provides the best service is probably going to be the most successful. I urge my clients to put together a game plan with goals, just as a football team or any sports team would do. I call operations the defensive team, sales and marketing the offensive team, and costing and pricing special teams.

I was asked to attend, as an observer, an LTL carrier's planning meeting to see how they put their budget and goals together for the upcoming year. The operations executive made his presentation, the sales executive made her presentation, and she was followed by the traffic and pricing executive. After they had completed their presentations, I asked all three to stand up. I proceeded to ask them if they had worked together on the budget and goals for the upcoming year. Guess what the answer was? Yep, you guessed it—the answer was no! The president of the company immediately said the meeting was over and asked them to make a plan together; another meeting would be scheduled.

A company must have a control system that will get everyone on the same page and aligned! If such a system isn't in place, there is a great risk of management by thrashabout. The main thrust of the stabilization stage is control system development and managerial accounting system development.

Financial Management

The basic thrust for financial management in the stabilization stage is providing better, more meaningful controls without all the accounting jargon. Keep it simple and communicate!

Putting in place a control system that gives you accurate information to the point that you can tighten or loosen the level of control needed at different points in the stage is critical. Managers have a tendency to begin with control that is too loose so the pushback from other managers and employees is not strong. That is a mistake. Initially the controls should be tight and uncomfortable for everyone. Part of the reason the company got into trouble in the first place is the culture of the company, so this is the stage when the new and improved culture must be implemented. If the culture does not change, you run the risk drifting back to the trauma stage. It is much easier to loosen controls once you are comfortable you have a new and improved culture of performance and accountability in place than it is to tighten them after starting out with loose controls. How you implement the controls and manage them is critical. It is important to remember that at all times we must treat everyone, both managers and employees, with dignity and respect.

In the trauma phase, the objective was simply to stop the bleeding and get to a cash-positive position, even at the expense of profit. This is the time to make certain you get away from running the company from a traditional income statement if the change wasn't made during the trauma stage. While the traditional EBITDA format is good for lenders and investors, you simply cannot manage your company from it. Dependence on the traditional income statement for managing the company is like driving a car forward by looking in the rearview mirror. A company must have a managerial accounting system that works in concert with the key operating controls used to manage the company on a daily basis.

An LTL carrier must ensure that an operating income statement for each terminal is available on a weekly basis. Running a company from a traditional income statement is ineffective; since it is generally not available until two to three weeks into the following month, you're always reacting to it. Game over by then, and you're probably on the way to losing another game. I encourage my clients to look at the year like a football season. A team plays 12 games, and a company has 12 months. Each month represents a game. A football game has 4 quarters, and a month has 4 weeks (some weeks might have a few days that fall into another month, but you still treat that week as quarter). Each week is an opportunity to make a winning play, and each month is an opportunity to add a game to the win column.

<u>Managerial Accounting</u>
As I noted earlier in this chapter, a company simply cannot be managed from traditional accounting statements. I know for a fact that managerial accounting does not exist in the majority of companies. In every company that has sought my help, I have found that there was either no managerial accounting system in place, or a managerial accounting system that provided inaccurate, incomplete, non-relevant information to the company's management. Senior management teams need to feel confident that they have reliable information that can be used for decision-making. What traditional accounting systems tell you is the bottom line; the balance sheet just fulfills regulatory requirements. Regulatory requirements and lender requirements for the accounting system should not be part of the numbers, nor contaminate the numbers required by the management team for day-to-day management of the company.

Some of the basic information that should be included in a managerial accounting system is outlined below. As we progress through the book, each element will be considered in more detail.

1. **Cost breakdowns** by major variable cost category, such as pickup and delivery (including fringes and variable equipment cost), dock/platform (including fringes), and linehaul (including fringes and variable equipment cost) should be included.

2. **Revenue and shipment count** per day for each terminal and the company as a whole should be included in the managerial accounting system.

3. **Customer profitability analysis and customer base analysis:** The company should analyze the potential of existing customers, and then build add-on volume from existing customers that are good for the company.

4. **Managerial accountability**: Each terminal manager and department manager must have information on every area for which they are responsible. For example, a terminal manager must have information on pickup and delivery capacity utilization, dock management, linehaul trailer utilization management, claims management, and revenue and shipment growth. This information should be rolled up to the head of the operations department.

5. **Pricing**: This is an area that needs to be more distinct and precise in the stabilization stage. Too much pricing is done "in the mix" and in this stage, pricing should be approached with a scalpel rather than with the meat ax used in the trauma stage. You should have offloaded the majority of your losers in the trauma stage. Now you want to make the best use of existing customers and markets. In this phase, aim to stabilize the pricing process for maximum contribution; you're pushing to build a more productive customer base. Rather than approach a customer with a general price increase for the entire account, approach the customer with pricing by lane. And on your bill-to accounts, push for price increases on particular customers rather than the entire bill-to account.

In the stabilization stage, the primary objective is to get everyone thinking profit. Teach your terminal managers how to run a business and make money, not just how to manage a terminal. This is not motivation, but rather helping people to understand the cost of operating inefficiencies, and to understand that you can't bring business on that operates at a loss and expect operations to make it profitable.

I tell my senior management clients that employees think they're dealing with monopoly money, that it's not real. They believe corporate has a huge money-making machine and when they need more money, like the federal government, they just print it. They do not understand the cost of money. In this phase it is senior management's responsibility to help employees to understand not only that they are dealing with real money, but also how their performance impacts the profitability of the company. The senior management team must open up the lines of communication and install a communication process that makes *all* employees feel needed and appreciated and that keeps them informed of the progress of the company and the reasons why decisions are made. Finally, you must reward their performance. Employees need to know you're going to share the success of the company with them and their loved ones. A later chapter dives into performance-based compensation. Don't skip ahead, though—that's why the book is titled *The LTL Carrier's Profitability Blueprint*.

This is the stage you must conquer to reach the back-to-growth phase. You cannot reach that next stage unless your employees are onboard with you and understand how their performance affects the growth and profitability of the company.

The Back-to-Growth Stage

In this stage you should be thinking about long-term development. You're not ready to run a marathon yet, but the company is stable enough to begin reinvesting for the future. The main thrust in this stage is to position the company for the next 20 years. The financial focus of this stage is positioning the company from a capital standpoint to support increased growth by building lender relationships, building cash reserves, and similar activities so the company doesn't run out of money.

Management will need improved marketing to support this vision. How is the company going to grow? Organically, or through acquisitions, or both? Internal investments in operations should be made in order to improve productivity and build capacity for growth. Capacity in this case not only means operational capacity, but also human resource capacity. Remember that human capabilities determine the level of financial capabilities, which determines the company's physical capabilities. In the stabilization stage, did you build your management team for the future? If not, you had better begin now. Unfortunately, some people only have the capacity to get the company to a certain point in its growth. It is imperative you evaluate your management team against your vision and strategy and ask the question, "Can my current team get us where we need to be?" The biggest limitation to growth is human capacity. If you have not already gone through this exercise, now is the time to do so.

In addition to the operations management practices in the two previous stages that we have already covered, two additional projects are added in this stage.

1. Develop specific objectives for the operations team, with specific goals and expectations in the leverage areas. In the stabilization stage, you initiated a culture change to position the operations department as a performance-based unit that also serves the customer. Think of the philosophy of the defensive unit on a football team: one of its major goals is to put the offense in a position to win. There are many statistics a coaching staff uses to improve performance, but the key statistic is scoring defense because if the opponent can't score, he can't beat you. The defense sets up the offense. The operations department sets up the offense (sales) by being the most efficient carrier in pickup and delivery, dock/platform operations, and linehaul trailer utilization, while providing the best service to the customer. By service I mean not only on-time delivery performance, but also pickups. You simply do not miss pickups. Period.

2. In order to accomplish operations goals, capital investment in human resources and systems is critical. The system must be one that can accurately measure capacity, capacity utilization, and productivity. It cannot rely on the tired old standby measurements, such as wages as a percent of revenue, stops per hour, pounds per man-hour, and so on. As we say in the South, that dog ain't gonna hunt! The costing system should be tied to the operations system, not the financial system.

Specific goals and objectives must be instituted to keep everyone focused and on the same page. I have worked with companies that have so many measurements they get confused about which are the important ones, so I encourage my clients to keep it simple. Remember to think of the operations department as the defensive side of the ball, sales and marketing as the offensive side of the ball, and costing and pricing as special teams. Those three departments must be aligned. I encourage companies to develop 8 to 10 measurements that will keep focus on objectives and improving performance. At the end of each week (the equivalent of a quarter), I suggest they grade themselves on their goals. There is no gray area: you either hit the goal or you did not. Calculate the percentage of achievement and trend the percentage on a chart. The objective is to see if you're getting better, if you've plateaued, or if you are moving backward. Just keep it simple.

This stage is really all about growth and profit improvement. Operations management's role in this stage is to set up the sales and marketing department for success. If senior management has done their job, they have provided the operations manager with a system that measures capacity and capacity utilization. Their job is to absorb new growth with capacity already in place. Doing this drives profit improvement, lowering variable cost as a percent of revenue and increasing contribution dollars. Of three legs on the stool—operations, costing and pricing, and sales and marketing—sales and marketing is now the first leg on the stool. The company must focus on increasing revenue growth to improve profitability by leveraging existing markets and existing customers and by building new markets.

As an example of how thinking shifts in this phase, let's turn to pricing strategy. In the trauma stage, the pricing strategy was to raise prices even at the expense of volume. In the stabilization phase, the pricing strategy was to stabilize the pricing department to improve contribution. In the back-to-growth phase, the strategy is to lower price to build share. If senior management has set up the operations department with the proper leadership and provided them with the proper measurement system, they will drive increased contribution dollars.

The sales and marketing strategy in the trauma stage was to eliminate customers that were draining cash from the company, while ensuring that new customers were winners. In the stabilization phase, the strategy was to increase contribution dollars through selective price increases for current customers and to add only new customers that are good for the organization, not necessarily in terms of profitability, but from a contribution and capacity standpoint. In this phase, the idea is to build share aggressively across all segments and markets within the company. In the back-to-growth stage, the company will invest heavily in promotion while lowering price strategically to build market share. Growth will occur organically, through acquisition, or a combination of both.

Summary

Earlier I noted that running a company is like riding a bicycle: You either keep moving forward or you'll fall down. The intent of this chapter to share with you, the reader, at 40,000 feet, how decline occurs and how, like a sick patient, companies must go through three stages, undertaking certain treatments in each phase to return to good health, or growth.

This chapter also sets us up to move forward with the Blueprint, which is the focus of this book. Obviously, the best way to stay healthy is to practice preventative medicine, taking care of your business so it does not enter a state of decline. The LTL Profitability Blueprint is designed to accomplish just that!

In Chapter 2, we'll talk about understanding the game.

CHAPTER 2

UNDERSTANDING THE GAME

"The key to ending management frustration is to have a managerial accounting system. That managerial accounting system should not be linked to the financial accounting system if it cannot avoid being contaminated by it. Measuring operational capacity and capacity utilization are paramount in understanding the business. Fundamentals are enduring; complexity is a competitive disadvantage."

—R. Sullivan

It is important to understand the game. In this chapter, we will discuss how important it is to:

1. Understand the key relationship: variable cost as a percent of revenue

2. Have a managerial variable/fixed income statement

3. Understand cost, volume, and contribution (CVC)
4. Understand the breakeven revenue point

Variable Cost and Revenue

To begin, let's define variable cost. For an LTL carrier, the definition of variable cost is costs that change with a change in volume or output. Fixed cost and overhead will not vary within a relevant range.

The carrier must control the quality and quantity of revenue and the variable cost used to handle that revenue because an LTL carrier is extremely capital intense. This capital intensity is driven by variable cost, which consumes 65 to 70 cents of each revenue dollar. Variable cost is determined by how well the carrier manages capacity in pickup and delivery, dock and platform, and linehaul trailer utilization. Those three categories comprise 93 to 95% of total variable cost. The remaining variable cost is property liability and property damage (PL/PD) insurance, claims less salvage, and hourly clerical cost.

Please look at the diagram below to understand what goes into the variable cost bucket. These categories may vary a little from carrier to carrier, but essentially these are the main sources of variable cost.

Transportation Profitability Group

Variable Cost

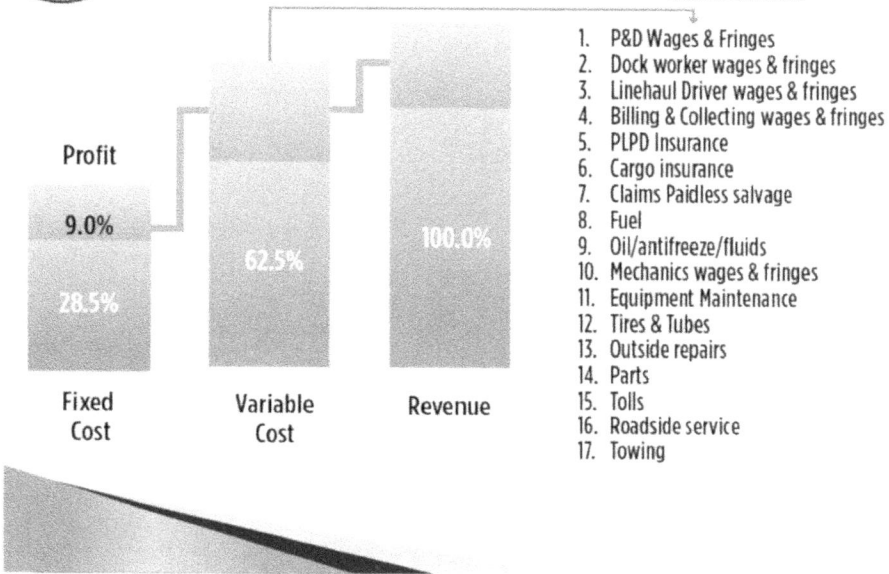

1. P&D Wages & Fringes
2. Dock worker wages & fringes
3. Linehaul Driver wages & fringes
4. Billing & Collecting wages & fringes
5. PLPD Insurance
6. Cargo insurance
7. Claims Paidless salvage
8. Fuel
9. Oil/antifreeze/fluids
10. Mechanics wages & fringes
11. Equipment Maintenance
12. Tires & Tubes
13. Outside repairs
14. Parts
15. Tolls
16. Roadside service
17. Towing

Profit 9.0%
28.5%
Fixed Cost

62.5%
Variable Cost

100.0%
Revenue

Now that we understand the components of variable cost, let's move forward in understanding the game!

The key relationship in a LTL carrier is the percentage of variable cost to revenue. Remember, a carrier should always focus on managing the "quality and quantity of revenue and the variable cost used to handle that revenue." We'll jump into that, but first let me suggest charting the key relationship and watching the trend.

For the LTL carrier, variable cost as a percent of revenue should be less than 70%. If variable cost as a percent of revenue is 70%, the company is probably breakeven at best. If variable cost is above 70%, the company is more than likely losing money. Ideally that percentage should be in the low to mid 60s. I have reviewed quite a few companies over the past 28 years, and I have found that fixed and semi-fixed expenses as a percentage of revenue generally run in the 27% to 32% range.

Imagine that an LTL carrier has three buckets. The first bucket is the revenue bucket. All revenue flows into the revenue bucket. The second bucket is the variable cost bucket; all the costs mentioned in the example above go into that bucket. The third and remaining bucket is the fixed cost bucket. All fixed, semi-fixed, and overhead cost goes into this bucket. Once those costs are covered, any remaining revenue rises above the fixed cost line and becomes profitability.

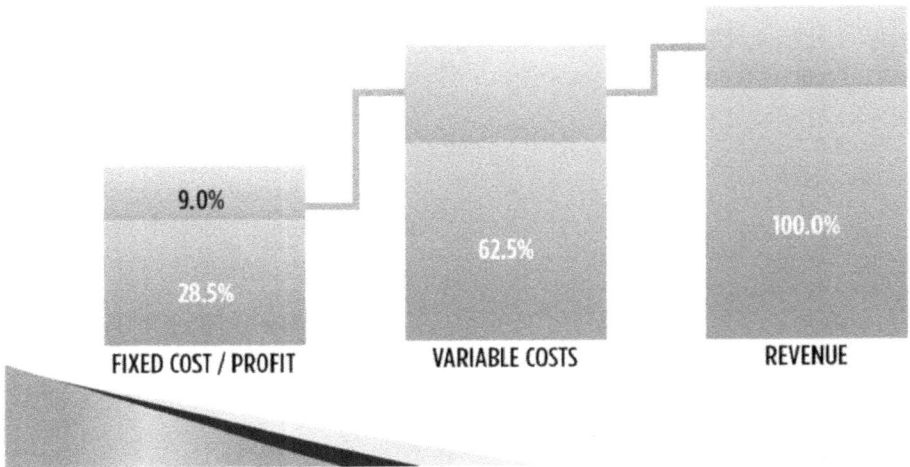

| FIXED COST / PROFIT | VARIABLE COSTS | REVENUE |

9.0%
28.5%
62.5%
100.0%

The key relationship for an LTL carrier is the relationship of variable cost to revenue. As you recall, variable costs are those costs that change with a change in output or volume. If variable cost rises at a higher level than revenue, the carrier has fewer "contribution dollars" left to flow over into the fixed-cost bucket. When that happens, profitability diminishes. If the rise in variable cost is not arrested, the carrier will find itself moving rapidly toward the trauma stage.

An LTL carrier will throw off cash faster than it can spend it if the carrier is run properly. Conversely, an LTL carrier will suck up cash exponentially if not run properly. As noted earlier, an LTL carrier is extremely capital intense and that intensity is driven by capacity in pickup and delivery, dock operations, and line-haul operations, which comprise 96% of total variable costs.

A common mistake in most costing systems is the use of "direct" costs, of which depreciation is one. The bank doesn't care if you move that piece of equipment; all they want is their payment each period. Also erroneously included are terminal manager and supervisor salaries, among various other fixed costs. In essence, the company is taking some fixed costs and treating them as variable.

Fixed cost is where you make your investments; you cover those investments by managing the relationship of variable cost to revenue.

Fixed costs are elements such as capital expenditures, salaries, rent, depreciation, and so on—costs that will be incurred whether any business is handled or not. While some can be eliminated, like salaries, they are costs that will not increase with an increase in volume.

The scenario I see when working with a carrier that is in the trauma stage or moving toward that stage is the relationship of variable cost to revenue has deteriorated and because of that, contribution dollars to cover fixed cost and overhead are reduced to the level where the carrier cannot cover its fixed cost and overhead. This is where the trouble begins. The cash crunch has arrived! The carrier will usually adopt a growth-for-growth's-sake strategy because they believe more revenue is needed. The carrier will usually lower the quality of pricing to attract more business.

A funny thing happens to revenue once it hits a terminal: It loses its identity. It becomes work and shipments that the terminal has to work across the dock and pick up and deliver. The terminal is also most likely using outdated, ineffective cost measurements, such as wages as a percent of revenue, stops per hour, shipments per hour, and pounds per man hour. Those are measurements "in the mix" and they cannot accurately measure capacity or productivity. Now, throw in the paradigms of supervisors that control the cost in the terminal and you have a volatile cocktail for disaster. When I say paradigms I am referring to the mindset supervisors have about how much work a driver can do and how much freight they can effectively move across the dock with current labor.

Since revenue loses its identity once it hits the terminal and becomes work, the supervisor will raise his hand and yell, "I need more trucks, more trailers, more drivers, and more dock workers." Hours will begin to rise and overtime will increase (not the good kind of overtime) and things will get worse. The level of the variable cost container will begin to rise at a faster rate than the level of the revenue container, contribution dollars will decline because variable cost is rising, and soon it's game over! You're done! When a player loses his legs in a game, we coaches would say, "he's done, stick a fork in him!" That is a good metaphor for not managing that key relationship. Hello Trauma stage!

The next thing the carrier in trouble tends to do is attack fixed costs. You can do that once, maybe twice, and get to breakeven or a little below, but the carrier always finds itself back in an unprofitable position; that is treating the symptom, not the problem. The problem is the variable cost-to-revenue relationship. Remember from Chapter 1 that the issue is not that leaders cannot solve their problem; it's that they cannot see their problem. They cannot see their problem because they are using outdated cost control methods that cannot measure capacity and capacity utilization, and they are using cost-based costing systems that are not aligned with operations and use operating ratio as their measurement for quality of revenue.

In Chapter 1 we studied breakeven revenue and the importance of understanding the calculation and watching the trend of that all-important number as an early warning signal. In this chapter, we will continue to study that number and its sensitivity, so we need to understand the key relationship in managing the profitability of an LTL carrier.

Companies must be efficient and productive in today's competitive environment. Traditional productivity measurements and traditional costing systems cannot measure capacity and capacity utilization. ***If you do not know the capacity in operations and capacity utilization, you DO NOT know your costs.*** But that's a topic another chapter. Let's get back to how the variable and fixed income statement can be used to better understand the business.

The Variable/Fixed Income Statement

When I install the TPG system and begin working with a company, the first task is to create a variable/fixed income statement. That's how important it is to the ability to see where a company is and the magnitude of the task ahead.

Revenue/Sales

Let's begin with revenue. There should be some distinctions between revenue sources. For example, interline/partner payout should be shown as a reduction in revenue, not a cost category on the income statement. The carrier should always show fuel surcharge revenue separately from freight or sales revenue so the quality of revenue delivered by the sales team can be measured. Your goal is to calculate net revenue so that an accurate revenue-per-shipment figure can be calculated. This is *extremely* important, so don't go any further until you understand why the carrier wants *its own* net revenue. We'll discuss this more when we get to variable cost and contribution dollars per shipment in the cost, volume, and contribution (CVC) section.

Variable Cost Categories

Generating a variable/fixed income statement makes that key relationship for profitability visible and becomes a tool that management can use to have better control over the company.

As a refresher, let's recall which categories are considered variable.

P&D drivers' wage and fringe costs are variable, as are linehaul drivers' wage and fringe costs. I would suggest creating two line items for those categories, one for

P&D drivers and one for linehaul drivers. Also, create a line for dock/platform workers' wages and fringes. We have a tendency to look at wages without considering the cost of fringes by category. Failing to consider those costs results in missing the impact—25% to 35% or more—fringe expense has on those areas. For example, if the base pay for a P&D driver is $19.00 and fringes are 28%, the cost of that driver for an hour is $24.32 an hour, not $19.00.

Set those three categories—wage and fringe costs for P&D drivers, linehaul drivers, and dock/platform workers—in a separate section and calculate a total for the three. Always show temporary labor for P&D separately from P&D wages and fringes. The same holds true for the dock. In linehaul, separate out purchased transportation.

Calculating Wages and Fringes for Pickup & Delivery, Dock, and Linehaul

Let's begin by looking a little deeper at the philosophy. Operations drives the variable cost of the company. You want this variable/fixed cost income statement to reflect the cost of operations as closely as possible. Therefore, your costing system should not use wage and fringe costs from the traditional income statement—too much flux and too many adjustments. For example, PTO (paid time off) can fluctuate dramatically during the summer and fall. Medical insurance and workers' compensation payouts can change as well, depending on how the carrier handles the payout.

Look at the wage and fringe calculation below, which is tied more closely back to the operations of the company and brings stability to the costing system. Tying this back to a format that more closely reflects the operations year brings stability to the costing system.

To calculate the base wage, I suggest using a weighted average. If you wish to take a more conservative approach, it is perfectly fine to use the highest wage per hour for the category and the base. Set categories that apply to your company. The objective is to use numbers that most accurately reflect a particular terminal. For example, holidays vary from company to company; I have run into companies that treat an employee's birthday as a day off. Workers' compensation rates vary from state to state. State income taxes also vary, and some states do not collect an income tax.

Mileage-Related Expenses

Next, I suggest including a section called "Mileage-related Expenses"—variable only! A company should know its variable cost per mile. This category includes items like fuel.

P&D Driver	ORD	Per Hour
Hourly Rate	$ 18.25	
Daily Wage	$ 146.00	
Weekly Wage	$ 730.00	
Annual Wage	$ 37,960.00	
Safety Bonus	$ -	$ -
Signing Bonus	$ -	$ -
Incentive	$ 900.00	$ 0.47
Vacation (10 Days)	$ 1,460.00	$ 0.76
Holiday	$ 876.00	$ 0.45
Bereavement	$ 292.00	$ 0.15
Sick Pay	$ 292.00	$ 0.15
Health ($300 * 12 Months)	$ 3,600.00	$ 1.87
Pension (12 Months)	$ -	$ -
Workers Comp.($10.00 per $100 Payroll)	$ 4,178.00	$ 2.17
Umemployment Insurance		
State (.0340 on 1ST $13,000)	$ 442.00	$ 0.23
Federal (.008 on 1St $7,000)	$ 56.00	$ 0.03
Social Security (.0620 on 1ST $113,700)	$ 2,534.56	$ 1.31
Medicare (.0145 No max)	$ 592.76	$ 0.31

FRINGE PERCENT		**30.20%**
FRINGE COST PER HOUR		**$ 7.90**
TOTAL COST FOR YEAR	**$ 53,183.32**	**$ 26.15**

Days in Year	365
Weekends	104
Holidays	6
Vacation	10
Sick Days	2
Bereavement	2
Other	0
Other	0
Total Non Productive Days Per Year	124
Total Productive Days Per Year	241
Work Hours Per Day	8.0
Productive Hours per Year	1,928

Let's talk fuel and fuel surcharge for a moment. Many companies have fuel surcharge (FSC) included in their revenue number on the income statement and net fuel cost. I suggest looking at this from a different perspective. Break out your fuel surcharge revenue and show it as a separate line item in the revenue section. You might label revenue without fuel surcharge as "Trade Revenue" or "Freight Revenue." Underneath that item, insert a line labeled "Fuel Surcharge Revenue." Using this format gives you a better view and understanding of revenue generated by your sales department. We now have our actual fuel expense, not net fuel adjusted for FSC. When you don't consider fuel separately, the picture gets a little muddy!

Now, back to the mileage-related line items. Include mechanics' wages and fringes for hourly paid employees only. If you have salaried personnel in maintenance, those costs would be included in the fixed cost section because their salaries would not change with a change in volume. On the other hand, if maintenance activity increases, hourly wages would increase as well.

Next you would have parts less any reimbursed warranty work, if you are under that type of program. Outside maintenance performed by vendors should also be included as a mileage-related expense, as should items like tolls, purchased transportation, oil and other fluids, towing expenses, tires, and tubes.

Equipment depreciation is not a variable expense. It falls under the fixed side because the note-holder doesn't care if you use the equipment or not; they want their fixed payment regardless. However, if you have leased equipment with a per-mile cost as part of the lease, that portion of the lease cost would be considered variable.

In this section you should include a line for total miles in P&D and linehaul, as well as purchased transportation. By dividing the total mileage-related cost by total miles, you are able to see your equipment cost per mile.

The example below gives per-day numbers. As I have noted, I recommend breaking the income statement down to per-day numbers to smooth out the difference in workdays per month.

TOLLS		(1,990)
TOLLS		4,972
DIESEL FUEL		11,544
FUEL SURCHARGE		3,114
PAYROLL MECHANIC		2,751
PAYROLL TAXES MECHANIC		346
FRINGES MECHANIC		282
OIL & GREASE		0
OIL WHITE FUEL		0
REPAIR PARTS - TRUCKS		1,630
REPAIR PARTS - TRAILERS		527
TIRES		1,019
TOWING CHARGES		296
TRUCK MAINTENANCE & REPAIR		745
TRAILER MAINTENANCE & REPAIR		146
OUTSIDE REPAIR SERVICES		0
SHOP SUPPLIES		448
HIGHWAY USE TAXES		268
IFTA TAXES		57
TOTAL MILEAGE REALTED		**26,154**
TOTAL MILES		**26,955**
VARIABLE COST PER MILE	$	**0.97**

Billing and Collecting Cost

Billing and collecting cost includes those hourly-paid employees' wages and fringes in the billing department, rating, collections/receivables, and customer service. Calculating billing and collecting cost allows a carrier to understand the cost per freight bill for getting the revenue into the company as a deposit. Simply take the wages and fringes for those areas and divide by bill count to get a transaction cost per bill. In the costing process, each freight bill will get a billing and collecting cost.

Insurance and Claims

The insurance and claims item is claims expense, less salvage, property liability and property damage (PL/PD) insurance, and cargo insurance. These insurance categories are tied to number of power units and revenue, which have variable cost. Insurance on fixed assets would fall under the fixed cost section. Sum up claims and insurance cost and divide that by total revenue to get insurance and claims (I&C) cost as a percentage of revenue. Each freight bill should be evaluated for insurance and claims cost as a percentage of the shipment revenue in per-day numbers.

FREIGHT CLAIMS	314
AUTO FLEET INSURANCE	1,305
CARGO INSURANCE	192
PROPERTY PACKAGE COVERAGE	99
GENERAL LIABILITY / PROPERTY	93
TOTAL INSURANCE & CLAIMS	**2,002**
INSURANCE & CLAIM PERCENT OF REVENUE	**1.71%**

In summary, the following categories reflect the variable cost of the company:

1. **Revenue**
   Trade Revenue or Freight Revenue
   Fuel Surcharge Revenue
   Interline/Partner Revenue (This would be a negative number)
   Sales Commissions (This would be a negative number)
   Total Revenue

2. **Wages & Fringes:**
   P&D Drivers
   Linehaul Drivers
   Dock/Platform
   Total Wages and Fringes

3. **Mileage-related Expenses:**
   Mechanic Wages and Fringes
   Fuel (Straight up)
   Oil and Fluids
   Parts
   Outside Repairs
   Shop Supplies
   Tolls
   Towing
   Tires
   Tubes
   Purchased Transportation
   Total Mileage-Related Expenses (Those are samples and may vary from company to company)
   Total Miles (P&D, Linehaul, Purchased Transportation)
   Equipment Cost per Mile

4. **Billing & Collecting**
   Wages & Fringes
   Total Freight Bills
   B&C Cost per Bill

5. **Insurance & Claims**
   Claims Expense
   PL/PD & Cargo Insurance
   Total I&C cost
   I&C Cost as a Percentage of Revenue

Total Variable Cost (Sum of 2, 3, 4, and 5)
Variable Cost as a Percent of Revenue (Total Variable Cost Divided by Total Revenue)
Contribution Dollars to Fixed and Semi Fixed Cost (Revenue Minus Variable Cost)

Contribution Margin Percent
(Contribution Dollars Divided by Revenue)

Revenue that is not consumed by variable cost leaves contribution dollars to cover fixed and semi-fixed costs. The section below should list all fixed and semi-fixed costs, including items like fixed salaries and fringes, rent, utilities, depreciation, equipment rents, professional and accounting fees, interest expense, management fees, office supplies, tariffs, entertainment, automobile expenses, and so on.

Total up your fixed and semi-fixed expense.
   Total Fixed and Semi Fixed Expense:
   Fixed and Semi Fixed Expense % of Revenue:
   Total Costs (Sum of Fixed and Variable):
   Operating Income (Revenue Minus Total Costs):
   Operating Ratio:

   Revenue per Shipment:
   Variable Cost per Shipment:
   Contribution Dollars per Shipment:

   Breakeven Revenue (Total Fixed Cost Divided by Contribution Margin Percent):
   Percent of Breakeven (Total Revenue Divided by Breakeven Revenue):

Now you have an income statement that gives you a better breakdown of the key relationships that you have control over, which will allow you to manage more

effectively. I also suggest adding a column next to the monthly numbers and calculate each line item on a per-day basis to compensate for the different workdays
per month. Looking at the numbers on a per-day basis gives you apples-to-apples
comparisons and the ability to track trends more accurately.

CVC (Cost, Volume, Contribution)

To gauge long-term trends, I like to look at cost, volume, and contribution (CVC)
trends on a per-shipment basis, as well as the breakeven revenue trend and breakeven
shipment trend. Of course we want see the contribution dollars per shipment growing and percentage of breakeven to be over 100% and trending upward. We do not
want to see the breakeven shipment count growing at a faster rate than revenue. As
noted earlier, a key metric I have found in every company is the relationship of shipment percent of growth to revenue percent of growth; if shipment percent of growth
is larger than revenue percent of growth, the company is heading for trouble. For
example, if shipment growth is up 14% and revenue growth is up 12%, that is not the
trend you want to see. Carriers should carefully monitor breakeven relationships and
percent of growth in shipment versus revenue.

The next key area to monitor is revenue per shipment, variable cost per shipment, and contribution dollars per shipment. Chart it, trend it, manage it! In
many cases I see the revenue per shipment line trending up, but the variable cost
per shipment line also climbing at the same angle. This is an indication to me that
the carrier does not understand how to control variable cost. These carriers usually wallow in mediocrity, hovering around breakeven or a 2- to 4-point profit
margin. These carriers, while a factor in the marketplace, really never become a
threat to the market leaders.

Another trend to watch for is revenue per shipment trending down and variable
cost per shipment trending up. This is an indication that the carrier is in a
growth-for-growth's sake mode, with no clue how to manage variable cost, and
will enter the trauma stage, if it is not there already.

A company should see the variable cost per shipment climbing at a much slower
rate and flattening out if it absorbs growth with current capacity or improving
productivity. Ideally, carriers should see an inverse relationship between the revenue-per-shipment trend line and the variable-cost-per-shipment trend line. If
that is the case, the contribution-dollar-per-shipment line will mirror the revenue-per-shipment trend line, increasing to provide greater coverage of fixed and
semi-fixed cost.

If the company is bringing on the right kind of revenue, and if operations is productive and efficient, the carrier should see revenue per shipment at a good level

(though it doesn't necessarily have to be increasing), and variable cost per shipment declining, generating higher contribution dollars per shipment. If shipment volume is increasing and that relationship is improving, the company will find itself taking money to the bank in a wheelbarrow!

As noted earlier, the major cost categories were segmented on the variable cost portion of the profit and loss statement (P&L). Those categories are called "variable" because as volume increases, so does variable cost. Every shipment carries a level of variable cost. Nothing rides free.

However, if the company is absorbing a percentage of the revenue increase with capacity already in place, total variable cost will not increase at the rate revenue is increasing. That is how you make money as an LTL carrier: You grow revenue and absorb with capacity in place, increasing contribution dollars to fixed cost and profitability. Remember that traditional productivity measurements do not provide the company with information about how much capacity they have in P&D and dock operations, and using those outdated measurements hinders managers from maximizing profitability.

Let's look at a real example of understanding CVC and managing the key relationship of variable cost to revenue.

		5 Months Later
Revenue per shipment	$140.90	$133.94
Variable cost per shipment	$ 95.95	$ 97.39
Contribution dollars per shipment	$ 44.95	$ 36.55
Fixed cost & overhead (per day)	$41,120	$42,001
Operating Ratio	98.46	105.94
Shipments to cover fixed & overhead	**915 ($41,120/$44.95)**	**1,149**

Recall that the key relationship for an LTL carrier is variable cost as a percentage of revenue. It is the quality and quantity of revenue and the variable cost to hand the revenue. Notice in the example above that revenue per shipment declined by $6.96 over the five-month period, while variable cost per shipment increased by $1.44. Over the same five-month period, contribution dollars per shipment declined by $8.40 per shipment. Profitability progressively got worse. The carrier went from a 98.46 operating ratio to a 105.94 operating ratio.

What I explain here and in the following section on breakeven revenue is what pushes carriers into the trauma stage. Notice that in the example, fixed cost per day increased a little, from $41,120 per day to $42,001 per day. Notice that the shipments needed to cover the fixed cost increased from 915 per day to 1,149 per day. **That is a necessary increase of 234 shipments per day, or a 25.6% increase in shipment count—just to cover fixed cost.**

In this situation, shipment count increases, the carrier is using outdated, ineffective cost control measurements on the variable cost side, and the carrier gets into a vicious cycle of chasing expenses with more revenue. Never works, never will! As shipment count increases, operations throws more dockworkers, more drivers, more trucks, and more hours at it. It's not their fault; it's the measurements used to control cost that have led the company astray. As a result, variable cost per shipment goes up, contribution dollars per shipment decline, and the company is on its way to the trauma stage.

Breakeven Revenue

Take a deep breath, clear your mind, and muster the highest level of concentration possible. I am about to share with you the most important early warning signal and the most misunderstood calculation in the industry.

When beginning work with a company, I always ask senior management about breakeven revenue and percent of breakeven they are at. When I don't get the deer in the headlights look, I get the answer that breakeven revenue is total expenses. The answer I'm given if total expenses per day are $200,000 is that $200,000 is the breakeven revenue. Nothing could be further from the truth.

Not understanding and watching this trend is what drives companies to the trauma stage.

Let's take a look at the numbers below from the same real-life carrier used above to demonstrate CVC.

Revenue less variable cost equals the contribution dollars remaining to cover the fixed cost and overhead of the company. Contribution margin is contribution dollars divided by revenue. If a carrier has $100,000 a day in revenue and $60,000 a day in variable cost, the carrier has $40,000 per day to cover fixed cost and overhead. The contribution margin is 40%.

Let's go back to our example. At the beginning, when the carrier's operating ratio was 98.46, its variable cost as a percent of revenue was 68.10. This tells us the out of every revenue dollar that came into the company, 68.1 cents was consumed by variable cost. So, out of every revenue dollar that came into the company, 31.9 cents remained (after covering variable cost) to cover $41,120 per day of fixed cost and overhead. The contribution margin was 31.9%. To calculate the breakeven revenue, take the fixed cost and overhead per day of $41,120 and divide that by .3190 (31.9% contribution margin):

$41,120/.3190 = $128,903.

The carrier's total expenses, fixed and variable, were $133,332. Actual revenue per day was $135,415. If we take actual revenue and divide that by breakeven revenue, the company was 105.1% of breakeven. At a revenue per shipment of $140.90, the company needed 915 shipments per day to break even.

You see, the reason this breakeven revenue is misunderstood is because you have to understand how the percentages of each revenue dollar are distributed. In this example, it takes 68.10 cents of every revenue dollar to cover variable cost, and only 31.9 cents of each dollar are left over to cover $41,120 dollars of fixed cost and overhead per day. Notice that 68.10 plus 31.90 equals 100. So 100% of each revenue dollar is identified.

Now, let's move ahead and see where the company stood five months later.
Five months later, the carrier had let variable cost as a percent of revenue increase from 68.1% of each revenue dollar to 72.71%. This tells us the out of every revenue dollar that came into the company, 72.71 cents was now consumed by variable cost. Thus, out of every revenue dollar that came into the company, only 27.29 cents remained (after covering variable cost) to cover $42,001 dollars per day of fixed cost and overhead. The contribution margin was therefore 27.29%. To calculate the breakeven revenue you must take the fixed cost and overhead per day of $42,001 and divide that by .2729 (27.29% contribution margin):

$42,001/.2729 = $153,906.

The carrier's total expenses, fixed and variable, were $133,919 (notice total expenses increased by $587 dollars per day). Actual revenue per day had dropped to $126,411. If we take actual revenue and divide that by breakeven revenue, the company was now at 82.14% of breakeven. With a revenue per shipment of $133.94, the company needed 1,149 shipments per day to break even.

As you see, a 4% increase in variable cost as a percent of revenue (from 68.10% to 72.10%) increased the breakeven point by 23%. That, my friends, is why carriers get into trouble. They begin chasing expenses with more revenue. This carrier's revenue per day decreased by $9,004 per day and variable cost only decreased by $294 per day.

Again, if an LTL carrier cannot measure capacity in operations, pickup and delivery, dock and linehaul trailer utilization, and the percent of utilization in each of those cost centers, the carrier does not know its costs of operations!

Not having the ability to measure capacity and capacity utilization, especially in pickup and delivery for the local and regional carriers prevents the carrier from adequately adjusting variable cost when the carrier is growing or contracting.

The Importance of Measuring Capacity and Capacity Utilization to Control Profitability

We now understand how important it is to:

1. Understand the key relationship: variable cost as a percent of revenue

2. Have a managerial variable/fixed income statement

3. Understand cost, volume, contribution (CVC)

4. Understand the breakeven revenue point

I hope you're beginning to understand how important it is to have a costing system that measures capacity in pickup and delivery, dock and linehual trailer utilization, and the percent of capacity utilization.

Let's move forward and see how having the ability to accurately measure capacity and capacity utilization can improve profitability. You will see three examples below. The first example illustrates how an increase in variable cost can negatively impact revenue, much like the example we used above with a real carrier. The second example shows the impact decreasing variable cost can have on profitability. The third example illustrates what an LTL carrier really wants to do: increase revenue and absorb the increase in revenue with capacity already in place.

Example #1: Increase in variable cost by 1%

PER DAY NUMBERS		ACTUAL PER DAY	PERCENT OF REV	1% INCREASE VAR COST	PERCENT OF REV
REVENUE	$	86,439	100.00%	$ 86,439	100.00%
SHIPMENTS		794		794	
VARIABLE COST	$	59,590	68.94%	$ 60,455	69.94%
CONTRIBUTION DOLLARS	$	26,849	31.06%	$ 25,984	30.06%
FIXED COST	$	26,564	30.73%	$ 26,564	30.73%
OPERATING INCOME	$	285	0.33%	$ (580)	-0.67%
OPERATING RATIO		99.67		100.67%	1.00%
REVENUE PER SHIPMENT	$	108.87		$ 108.87	
VARIABLE COST PER SHIPMENT	$	75.05		$ 76.14	$ 1.09
CONTRIBUTION PER SHIPMENT	$	33.81		$ 32.72	$ (1.09)
BREAKEVEN REVENUE	$	85,521		$ 88,369.93	$ 2,848
PERCENT OF BREAKEVEN REVENUE		101.1%		97.81%	-3.3%

Allowing variable cost to increase 1%, from 68.94% of revenue to 69.94% of revenue, drove an $865-per-day negative turn. Notice the breakeven point declined 3.29% because the contribution margin dropped from 31.06% to 30.06%. That 1% increase in variable cost increased the breakeven point by 3.29%.

Example #2: Decrease in variable cost by 1%

PER DAY NUMBERS		ACTUAL PER DAY	PERCENT OF REV	1% DECREASE VAR COST	PERCENT OF REV
REVENUE	$	86,439	100.00%	$ 86,439	100.00%
SHIPMENTS		794		794	
VARIABLE COST	$	59,590	68.94%	$ 58,727	67.94%
CONTRIBUTION DOLLARS	$	26,849	31.06%	$ 27,712	32.06%
FIXED COST	$	26,564	30.73%	$ 26,564	30.73%
OPERATING INCOME	$	285	0.33%	$ 1,148	1.33%
OPERATING RATIO		99.67		98.67%	-1.00%
REVENUE PER SHIPMENT	$	108.87		$ 108.87	
VARIABLE COST PER SHIPMENT	$	75.05		$ 73.96	$ (1.09)
CONTRIBUTION PER SHIPMENT	$	33.81		$ 34.90	$ 1.09
BREAKEVEN REVENUE	$	85,521		$ 82,858.17	$ (2,663)
PERCENT OF BREAKEVEN REVENUE		101.1%		104.32%	3.2%

In this example, decreasing variable cost by 1% improved operating income from $285 per day to $1,148 per day. A 1% decrease in variable cost increased operating income by 302.8%. Now this company is building operating leverage, and the breakeven point improved from 101.1% of breakeven to 104.32% of breakeven, a 3.2% improvement. All this improvement was driven by decreasing variable cost, which lowered variable cost per shipment and increased contribution dollars per shipment.

Example #3: Increasing revenue and absorbing revenue with capacity already in place

PER DAY NUMBERS		ACTUAL PER DAY	PERCENT OF REV	1% INCREASE REVENUE	PERCENT OF REV
REVENUE	$	86,439	100.00%	$ 87,303	100.00%
SHIPMENTS		794		798	
VARIABLE COST	$	59,590	68.94%	$ 58,717	67.26%
CONTRIBUTION DOLLARS	$	26,849	31.06%	$ 28,586	32.74%
FIXED COST	$	26,564	30.73%	$ 26,564	30.43%
OPERATING INCOME	$	285	0.33%	$ 2,022	2.32%
OPERATING RATIO		99.67			
				97.68%	-1.99%
REVENUE PER SHIPMENT	$	108.87			
VARIABLE COST PER SHIPMENT	$	75.05		$ 109.40	
CONTRIBUTION PER SHIPMENT	$	33.81		$ 73.58	$ (1.47)
				$ 35.82	$ 2.01
BREAKEVEN REVENUE	$	85,521			
PERCENT OF BREAKEVEN REVENUE		101.1%		$ 81,127.72	$ (4,394)
				107.61%	6.5%

What the carrier really wants to do is increase revenue and absorb that increase with capacity (cost) already in place. In order to do that, the carrier must have a costing system that can measure capacity and capacity utilization. Notice the 1% increase in revenue absorbed with capacity already in place dropped variable cost as a percent of revenue from 68.94% to 67.26%, or a reduction of 1.68%. The quality of revenue improved, and revenue per shipment increased from $108.87 to $109.40, or $0.53. However, because operations absorbed the increase in revenue with capacity already in place, variable cost per shipment dropped ($1.47). So between the two, contribution dollars per shipment improved by $2.01 per shipment. This drove operating income up from $285 dollars per day to $2,022 dollars per day. That is an increase in operating income of 609.5%. The breakeven point improved from 101.1% of revenue to 107.61%.

Understanding the Game

As a college football coach, I had to understand the game, including the leverage points and the enduring fundamentals. I had to become a student of the game if I wanted to continue to achieve at a level that benefitted the team, school, players, and my fellow coaches. If you don't understand the game—and the game is ever changing—you'll be left behind and your value to your organization will diminish. If you understand and apply this chapter's concepts, you now have a much better understanding of the game and will increase your value to your organization.

I taught my defensive linemen to step and strike when the ball was snapped. It all began with that. Never take a hit: deliver the hit. Understanding this chapter and the importance of being able to measure capacity and capacity utilization is the equivalent of understanding the importance of stepping and striking and delivering the hit, not taking it from your competition.

Also, you now are beginning to see that there really is a Blueprint to Profitability!

CHAPTER 3

The Barrier of Complexity

How we live is so different from how we ought to live that he who studies what ought to be done rather than what is done will learn the way to his downfall rather than his preservation.

Niccolo' Machiavelli – The Prince

A chapter titled "The Barrier of Complexity" appeared in my first book, *The Formula: Building Competitive Advantage*. In the years since its publication, many people have approached me to say that the chapter really hit home for them, and in several cases changed their lives. Others have told me that when they read the chapter, they felt as if I knew them personally. For those reasons, I decided an updated version of the chapter based on my continued experience would be an appropriate addition to this book.

I wrote this book to give you, a leader of an LTL carrier, a path to follow, a blueprint that will help you improve the performance and profitability of your company. If you are not already up against the barrier of complexity, at some point you will be. It is inevitable. How you and your organization respond to that moment defines you and your company.

Do you remember the movie *Groundhog Day* starring Bill Murray? If you cannot break through the barrier of complexity, both you and your organization will feel as though you are repeating the same day over again, and that feeling will continue until you break through.

One of the reasons companies, and leaders, fail to break through the barrier is management's extremely high tolerance level. In some cases I have found management thinks it is much easier to maintain the status quo because the pain of change is too great. I read a book by Tony Robbins some years ago in which he wrote that people will do more to avoid pain than they will to gain pleasure. I have found that to be spot on! Although life would be much more pleasurable after breaking through the barrier, the pain of doing so appears much greater, so managers keep hitting their heads against the barrier. However, once the pain becomes too intense, guess what? That's right: They will begin changing and try to break through, working to eliminate management by thrashabout.

After this chapter we will move into the "how to" portion of the book. To be successful, a leader must make the personal commitment to change, a personal commitment to continue to learn and grow in order to achieve at a high-level performance. To break through the barrier of complexity requires a change in the company's culture, starting with leadership.

> *"You don't turn people around; they turn themselves around. Create the environment, and people adapt. If [new] leadership is strong, those people who are really sensitive to good leadership will recognize it quickly and change their ways. Without a strong leader, companies fall apart a lot faster".*
>
> —Frank Grisanti

Eagle or Dinosaur?

In my line of work, I classify carriers as either Type 1 or Type 2. Type-1 carriers rarely rise above a level of poor performance; one doesn't hear too much about them, because their competitive impact is so negligible. Type-2 carriers' challenge is to maintain a leading position. The principal danger for these kinds of carriers is becoming sluggish and losing touch with the marketplace, customers, and people.

I place carriers into four categories: Leader, Competitor, Follower, and Dropout.

A *leader* is like the *eagle*: It soars high above all other birds, dominating and prospering with strength, size, and keen vision. A *competitor* is like the *hawk*: It tends to survive on a lower level than the eagle, yet has enough potential to be a factor in the marketplace. A *follower* is like the *turtle*, surviving on the ground in mundane mediocrity. The focus of this kind of carrier's leadership is *to avoid losing money*. A *dropout* is like the *dinosaur*, guaranteed to become extinct.

As you can see, these four categories differ most strikingly in their prospects for the future. However, to identify the position of carriers, I combine market position with the financial position of the company.

MARKET POSITION

		HEALTHY	WEAK
FINANCIAL POSITION	**HEALTHY**	Leader (Eagle)	Competitor (Hawk)
	WEAK	Follower (Turtle)	Dropout (Dinosaur)

Eagles, the market leaders in their operating area, have future-oriented leadership, a healthy product to sell, and the strongest financial position thanks to overwhelming financial resources. Carriers that exhibit these qualities are virtually guaranteed a prosperous future. They will use their financial strength to develop both new markets and future-oriented leaders. The financial pitfalls that normally await carriers with weaker human and financial resources pose little threat to the eagle.

At the opposite end of the spectrum are the dinosaurs. Their future is dismal. Any company in this worst category is not only selling an inferior product, but also has neither the leadership nor the financial strength to produce anything better. Yet no company is born a dinosaur. And none is formed to sell worthless products, or created in a financially unpromising situation. The path that leads to the dinosaur reputation this kind of carrier richly deserve starts with a past-oriented leadership that ignores the increasing complexity and competitiveness of the industry. Then, the company's financial position is left to deteriorate until it reaches a culminating point where regularly declining margins throw the leadership into a quagmire of indecision and confusion. This kind of company allows itself to become non-competitive.

The remaining carriers, hawk and turtle, have one weak and one healthy characteristic. A competitor is a financially healthy company whose leadership is more past-oriented than that of the industry leader. This translates into a relatively weak market position, even though low debt and a good asset base may dispel any immediate threat to survival. Finally, the follower is simply not designed for the 21st century. It manages to survive, but threatens to sink to the level of the dropout at any time.

In any given market, there is room for two or three players at the top, or the market leaders (eagles). Any company below that level—hawk, turtle, or dinosaur—may do well in good times, but in leaner times profits will fall to a level that reflects its poorer performance and inefficiencies. The performance of these Type-2 companies—consisting essentially in fighting for what is left of the market—is sluggish because the companies suffer from a number of leadership and control defects. The first signs of decline appear when a number of negative internal and external events strike simultaneously.

Looking Beyond the Surface

Psychology is critical to business success. Keeping your critical faculties alive at all times, however comfortable the situation may feel, is crucial to business survival. As a person who habitually looks beyond the surface of everything, I know how important it is to have a questioning mind. Questions can be a powerful vehicle for improvement and ultimate success in business. In view of their importance, here are some good preliminary questions to ask about your business:

> What do you need to do to achieve or exceed your goals?
>
> Are your goals challenging, yet attainable?
>
> Are you making it easy for your customers to do business with you?
>
> Are you treating your customers with the respect they deserve?
>
> Are you managing your capacity each day as well as you should?
>
> What is your sales focus?
>
> How well are you developing your people?
>
> Do you ever ask yourself who you are, what you are here for, or what lies ahead for you?

If you are in the habit of posing future-oriented questions like these, are you also answering them to your satisfaction?

At a certain point, these questions or similar questions will arise in every discerning and even undiscerning mind. In this chapter, I will share with you my views about *the exact point* at which this occurs. That's the point where a company is poised either to continue moving forward or to stagnate and decline. This point determines whether you will continue in a state of obscure mediocrity, or move forward into a magnificent awakening.

When you hit it, you will question yourself because, as I wrote in Chapter 1, an organization may be forgiven for pausing briefly before taking a new direction, but never for standing still. It is moving either forward or backward. That's just part of the natural scheme of things.

A more incisive way to state this "law," so to speak, is that an organization will either move forward or the distance between it and the market leaders will widen. From this angle, *the point* I am referring to is also the *barrier of complexity*. Whether or not a company breaks through this barrier depends entirely upon leadership. If leadership is past-oriented, the company will not break through the barrier. It may survive, but only in palpable mediocrity, and it will continue to be at risk.

Let's take the first step of our journey with this adage:

> ## Most companies lose money trying to avoid losses.

As a president, CEO, or senior-level manager responsible for bottom-line profitability, do you think more about ways to avoid losing money or ways to make money? There is a tremendous difference between the two. Are you managing the areas on your P&L and using the right tools to build operating and financial leverage into your business, or are you managing them in a manner that diminishes operating and financial leverage? Just answering this question will go a long way to placing you on the right side of that great divide separating past-oriented from future-oriented leaders.

If your company has future-oriented leaders, or at least has made the decision to install future-oriented leaders, it will break through the barrier and move on to the next level. This is a continuous process, and in order to maintain forward momentum, the organization's leadership must be fully committed to learning, growing, and achieving. This commitment is what makes the leaders of the company either future- or past-oriented. It is that simple. Everything depends on it.

I know CEOs who routinely make their decisions based on cost, with little or no consideration of opportunity. Without exception, however, their businesses trudge along in sheer mediocrity. Why do you suppose that is? I would say it has everything to do with mindset. Making money has a strong emotional element that we would be foolhardy to ignore. *Most companies intent on avoiding losses end up losing money* because they overlook the psychological dimension of their decision-making.

I have known several companies of this ilk. They have been marginally profitable and will continue to be marginally profitable. They remind me of turtles. Turtles were not made for the 21st century, but somehow they manage to survive, if survival means achieving no more than a delicate balance between internal and external forces. The longevity of this group does not rest on the fearless psychology of learning they will need to create a prosperous future for themselves and their employees. These companies are nothing more than hangers on.

Are you beginning to see how psychological the business of making money can be? I know many presidents and CEOs of successful companies. Sure, they spend their time thinking about how to make money, but they focus on providing superior service to the customer and on building a strong financial position. They purchase or develop new technology that facilitates competitive advantage and they enter new markets that build synergies. They understand the business they are in. They know their costs. Their attitude virtually guarantees prosperity and market leadership is for them. They are eagles because they hire the talent they need to build their position as market leaders. Eagles take the resources available to them to develop leaders and employees, and they rely on financial strength to enter markets already developed by competitors. The financial pitfalls looming on the horizon for most other organizations pose little threat to them. Like the eagles of the wild, they soar high above every other species in their environment.

To repeat: *Most companies lose money trying to avoid losses.* Can you see the difference between ways to avoid losing money or ways to make money now?

We are what we think. If you are always thinking about avoiding losses, what you don't have, or the position you do not occupy, what could really matter beyond losses and poverty? Let me put it another way. In a business meeting, which of two people has the real power? The one who wants nothing from the other, of course.

You're probably saying: He is just trying to pump me up, trying to motivate me. While I hope my words will have a salutary effect on your motivation, I know exactly how limiting working on motivation alone could be. I, too, went to seminars, read books, and listened to tape programs. I don't mind confessing to you that I felt so high and pumped up they had to peel me off the ceiling. But personal motivation can plummet as quickly as it can soar. It is not a constant factor and for that reason cannot be the answer we are looking for.

What then is the answer?

Leadership That Understands

If we are not after motivation and we are not after knowledge as the sole psychological elements of success in business, only understanding is left. I don't claim to know all the answers, but understanding is fundamental to the formula I am exploring in this book. Over the years, we learn that the more we think we know, the more we realize we don't know. That's the practical, time-honored sense of *understanding* I want to convey to you. Time reinforces the truths we learn in the course of practical living by teaching us a further truth: *understanding opens our minds and keeps us from sinking into a defensive or protective mindset, which can snatch prosperity right out of our hands.*

There are many corollaries to this definition of understanding. For instance, one of them is, "To change others we must first change ourselves." I certainly did not coin this magnificent saying, whose meaning borders on the spiritual. Just think of the power this idea can bring to a diligent business leader.

> *To change others we must first change ourselves.*

Leadership, I suppose, has always required a spiritual, forward-looking bent, in business as in every other human endeavor. How could anyone expect to lead the people who depend on them to ultimate success without a modicum of personal awareness of the principles upon which they are operating? Changing others requires changing these principles, should they prove unworkable or self-serving.

So, what are *your* principles? Do you lead your organization according to past-oriented or future-oriented principles?

Giving an honest answer to these questions should reveal something about your barrier of complexity. We all experience this barrier from time to time, though without truly understanding how or why it arises. Its causes are closely tied with many patterns of leadership I now consider to be waning but which have not completely disappeared. In our industry, the old style of leadership and the paradigms it has developed are quintessentially bureaucratic. Most of us are steeped in them. There was a time when that style of management worked relatively well. However, the increasing complexities of the marketplace have rendered the hierarchical approach ineffective. Organizations have become much flatter than at any time in history, so much so that leadership is on the cusp of the greatest change in modern times. At every level, leaders feel the pressure to be more entrepreneurial in the way they lead their organizations.

All these conditions favor the emergence of a new type of leader armed with the understanding that companies must limit their bureaucratic structures if they are to grow and prosper. This new leader knows that the bureaucratic approach generates complexity, which in turn slows a company's future response to change rather than enhancing control, as expected. Bureaucracy's only outcome is multiple layers of "specialists" in the guise of "staff," who draw more and more resources away from the line managers' primary task of making money for the firm. In the LTL industry, this forces service centers to throw layer on top of layer just to comply with the requirements handed down by the corporation. Needless to say, this activity impedes their ability either to build or to maintain their competitive advantage.

The proper leadership response to complexity is simplicity, which implies looking at things differently from how my generation of leaders has been taught. At every level, particularly the service center, leaders have to learn how to run a business, not just manage a service center. When subordinating themselves to the service centers, corporate staff and senior management must provide the necessary resources and advice, and reduce the number of directives they issue.

However, our industry is not yet at the level it should be with respect to leadership. Companies that make the necessary transition first, before their competitors, should enjoy a tremendous advantage over the competition. I have no doubt that making the transition will be a decisive factor in those companies' success.

These then are the stakes. In the future, leaders will be forced to seek a different kind of knowledge and to develop a different set of attitudes, skills, and habits than those current today in the industry. They must condition themselves to take up a habit of learning if they expect to grow and achieve. It makes all the difference in the world because companies, like people, go through various stages of growth. Human beings begin their lives as helpless infants and move through each stage until they reach a point where growth slows down and then stops. Some make it through a single stage and then grow no more. Others are able to pass through every stage of life. In fact, some people never stop growing, even in their twilight years.

Companies stop growing and lose their competitive edge because of the sheer weight of complexity built up in the course of transacting and problem solving. There are obligations to fulfill, requirements to be met, meetings to take part in, reports to complete, knowledge to acquire, skills to hone, and relationships to begin or to build. All this increases complexity to a point where it is difficult to do all that needs to be done and still expect prosperity. That's when personal or corporate growth stops, performance stagnates or worsens, and capability falls.

It is the point I call the "Barrier of Complexity."

Understanding Counterproductive Work

Every animate and inanimate organism encounters a barrier of complexity at some stage of its life—even a teenager can hit the barrier. All that the barrier of complexity implies is that no further growth is possible until a way is found to simplify the present. Success may open the way for renewed growth.

There are leaders who, understanding the gist of their experience and achievements in a preceding stage of growth, can create a state of simplicity that takes their organizations to the next stage. Whether the driver of change is the leader or the company as a whole, this is what it means to be the best. But the defining characteristic of being the best is a dynamic capacity rather than a static quality. Being the best means learning how to convert the knowledge gained through experience into an *understanding* that can move the organization to ever-higher levels of achievement.

The fallacy we have all been taught is that when the going gets tough, you have to work harder and longer to make it through the rough period. This strategy does not work. Even in the situations where it appears to work, the improvement is, at best, short lived. Working harder and longer *as a reflex* can be counterproductive.

I have seen this attitude in practice in many companies and among managers at every level. Despite their heroic struggles, there is a barrier that they simply cannot breach. Crisis sets in when the conditioned response to work harder and longer to break through the barrier becomes too intrusive. The way to break through the barrier is to work *smarter*. The smartest leaders have learned to extract the proven methods of experience, those that are productive or have made sense, and to throw away the rest. That, in short, is the simplification process!

A barrier of complexity may occur naturally because a previous set of goals has already been achieved and a new set of goals is needed. Goals push us forward; we grow so long as something external impels us to do so. Therefore, when a company hits the barrier, a new set of beliefs and strategies are needed, but these new ideas must always be tempered by experience and knowledge. Better thinking, not more effort, holds the key to genuine growth.

So, think carefully about where you are right now. Do you have a sense that something ought to be driving you forward, that everything is not all right, that you should be doing more?

These are natural questions to ask. We grow because something greater than us or what we possess pushes us to grow. By nature we seek achievement levels higher than those we occupy; they keep driving us forward. But there is more to it than that. Embarking on a new set of goals tends to *liberate* us from our previous growth stage and we begin to see the success we aspire to. Liberated, we feel freer to act more productively. The more *efficient* we are, the likelier our success. But once the new stage is reached, the very goals that had impelled us forward now begin to entrap us. This is when complexity sets in to hinder further progress, and no amount of effort will lift you from your predicament if you cannot think smarter or act more efficiently.

I am a good illustration of this principle. I am not divulging any hidden secret about my successes and failures, and I hope in the future you will be able to use your own experiences as an example as well. After all, leaders, like coaches, should be prepared to share knowledge with each other because doing so moves us all forward.

I had some pretty lofty goals in my 20s. I wanted to be the youngest service-center manager in my company and move into a senior management position within ten years of becoming a service-center manager. I wanted to own a business and help others understand the game. Motivated and extremely focused, I achieved my goal.

Because of my personal commitment to continue to learn and grow to achieve at higher levels, I have the pleasure of helping leaders and companies to become stronger, more knowledgeable, and to better understand their business. With an initial goal like that, I asked myself, what else do you need to create the next opportunity? That opportunity would present itself when the time came, or so I thought. When that did not transpire, I wondered why. Instinctively, I thought that achieving my goals had created a kind of block that prevented me from going further. So caught up was I in the *doing* that I lost sight of my broader vision and failed to prepare myself for the next level of goals.

In other words, I tried *to do everything for* everybody, not realizing that it was more important *to be someone to* them. Think about this for a moment.

Having achieved my goals, I lost my drive and focus. Thanks to the tremendous effort it took to reach my short-range goals, I reached intellectual burnout at a relatively early age—in my 30s— and didn't understand what had happened to me. All I knew was that I deeply disliked the pit I had found myself in emotionally and psychologically.

Escaping the Pitfalls of Success

I am more than happy to share with you how I liberated myself. The goals I had set and achieved impelled me to develop specific relationships, a specific organizational structure, and specific personal habits destined to take the service center

I was managing to a higher level of financial success. I felt no need to jettison my entire structure, my relationships, or my habits just to accommodate some vague personal notions about the need to develop a higher set of goals for myself. As time went on, though, success clearly became more difficult to achieve. By the time I hit the barrier, I was working harder and longer hours than ever before, and expected my supervisors and employees alike to do the same. We managed to score some short-lived successes, but the frustration grew and I had to seek answers.

As a manager, I valued the set of relationships I had developed. To me, people were the company's most important asset. However, I am the first to confess their propensity to be the greatest liability too. I learned the hard way that the goals you set are absolutely meaningless without the right people in place to execute your action plans. People can bring great success to a company (and a leader) just as easily as they can bring abject failure.

We all have our own beliefs about the human condition. One belief suggests that human beings are basically good, not just because "they done good" but, because they were "made that way." That's the belief I accept. I have not forgotten that human vacillation is part of the natural order. But human potential is the pith that a company needs to grow. We rely on it for the most elementary progress.

Poor leaders, though, can benefit neither from the potential of employees nor from their own potential. They can only create an atmosphere of defensiveness and poor performance that ultimately pervades the whole organization. I have learned that no matter how good the organization, some bad players will hang onto their jobs because they can't do anything else. Others are so inefficient they know they might have to work somewhere else; still others simply are in over their heads. Obviously, leaders want to help their people succeed, and sometimes that means putting them in positions where they can succeed. I learned the hard way that it was better to remove the few inefficient people from leadership roles than to force the many with the human potential I needed to suffer for their actions.

My first realization was that new goals require new relationships, structures, and personal habits. Reaching for a higher level demanded that I learn how to surround myself with the kind of people who knew how to behave at ever-rising levels of achievement.

The second thing I realized was that my new goals required different kinds of support structures—in other words, *expertise*. I had to attract new skills and knowledge. When I talk about new structures this is precisely what I mean, not more bureaucracy.

My third discovery was the need to think differently, to communicate differently, and to act in a different way because I was working at a higher level. My operating environment was changing, essentially becoming more complex. Yet I had to ensure that a state of simplicity prevailed throughout the organization. I knew that clutching my old ways of communicating, thinking, and acting—which, I might add, were perfectly appropriate for earlier stages of growth—would not achieve the desired transition to a higher level.

In an environment of rapid change, effective leaders must assume personal responsibility to seek personal growth. There is little alternative. When everything is moving around at the same time, the barrier is an irreducible fact of life. Even if you were the best at what you did five years ago, what you do now has to be different. At the start of my management career, when I was busy setting my goals, I thought that mastering certain skills could help me develop habits that would send me to the top. What I failed to realize was that even though the environment was constantly changing, I had barely adjusted to it. When you see this lack of adjustment, you know you've reached the barrier.

What if one could go through all of the work to overcome the barrier of complexity and still have fun doing it? My short answer is that no one likes to be part of a marginally profitable or losing team. To my mind, putting fun into your team's work means emphasizing hard work and the satisfaction that comes from being recognized as the best of the best!

Granted, needs vary widely from place to place and situation to situation. It is difficult, within the covers of a book, to describe everything leaders could do to adjust attitudes. My advice is to be creative. Beside that, there are some fundamentals you may want to communicate to your people that will get you started. Just make sure your subordinates understand you are looking for solutions to problems. They must understand that they should not scoff at creative solutions, but at the lack thereof. Let them know that you are well aware that mistakes will occur, but as long as the mistake is correctable, it is not serious. There is no progress without risk.

These are the elementary values to provide a positive framework within which to create a winning environment that enables you to attack your problems.

Summary

Understanding the barrier of complexity is the first ingredient in the recipe for growth. Don't fear it, but understand it; by understanding it you conquer it. If every department and service center is staffed with people who know how to cross the barrier, then the entire organization will know how to do it. A dinosaur's leadership will not understand how to do this, and a turtle's leadership is adept enough at survival to follow the competitor or industry leader; it recognizes and emulates some of the tactics, if not the strategies of the eagle and hawk, but has neither the creativity nor the courage to develop on its own.

The competitor (hawk) understands the rule of the game played out at the eagle (or market leader) level, but it hasn't yet the courage to change the rules of the game or to set new standards—which, after all, is the secret to gaining competitive advantage. You need to change the rules of the game as the game changes itself. Eagles excel at this, which is why they are market leaders. They have learned how to break through the barrier of complexity, one of the most important skills that a leader needs to move his or her company to the next level.

CHAPTER 4

PICKUP AND DELIVERY CAPACITY MANAGEMENT

The test of an organization is the spirit of performance

—**Peter Drucker**

Understanding the Game

If you are a local or regional carrier that provides next day or two-day service, you make your money in pickup and delivery (P&D). If you're a long-haul carrier, you're leaving millions of dollars on the table if you're not intensely focusing on P&D capacity and capacity utilization. Measuring capacity and capacity utilization in P&D is difficult to do because there are so many variables. It's relatively easy to measure capacity in linehaul, isn't it? You simply inspect the linehaul trailer visually and note the weight of the trailer and you can determine if the trailer is at 70% capacity or 60% capacity.

In P&D, it's simply not that easy. You can't look at a P&D trailer and determine capacity and capacity utilization. Now, you might look at the trailer and say, "It's got 26 skids on it," or "It is 80% full from a visual standpoint," but that doesn't mean that unit is full from a capacity and productivity standpoint. There are many variables that must be quantified to determine capacity and utilization on a P&D run. For example, how many miles is the P&D trip: 100 or 300? A driver who has to drive 300 miles does not have the time to do as much work as a driver who only drives 100 miles. Thus, capacity is different for those two runs. How many hours does the driver work in a day? A driver working 11 hours needs a different workload than a driver working 7 hours. In what geographic area is the trip? It takes longer to drive 100 miles in Philadelphia than it does in Hazleton, PA. Length of the trip, driver workload, and geography are a few of the variables that must be quantified in order to determine the capacity or capacity utilization of a P&D run and P&D operation within a terminal.

Outdated Productivity Measurements Cannot Measure Capacity

The measurements in use today perpetuate inefficiencies and increase operating cost. Measurements such a stops per hour, bills per hour, pounds per man-hour, and the all-time favorite, wages as a percent of revenue, simply do not even come close to being effective measurements of capacity and productivity. For example, given the wacky rates out there, you could have a 1200-pound shipment 10 miles from the terminal and an identical 1200-pound shipment 100 miles from the terminal, and both would have the same revenue. Using wages as a percent of revenue as a measurement of capacity and cost leaves a lot to be desired, doesn't it?

If a carrier can't measure capacity and capacity utilization in P&D, it cannot know its true cost and will not know how much additional work (which brings revenue with it) it can absorb in the terminal and company. As we discussed in earlier chapters, one of the major keys to building long-term, sustainable profitability in an LTL carrier is growing revenue and absorbing that revenue with capacity already in place. That is how you build operating leverage into the company.

Take a look at the illustration below. It shows that traditional methods of cost control are ineffective and even unfair to use in evaluating driver and supervisor performance.

| | Less Than Truckload | | | | Truckload | | | | |
	Stops	Shipments	Handling Units	Weight	Stops	Shipments	Handling Units	Weight	Drops Picks
Trip 1	12	21	150	30,000	0	0	0	0	0
Trip 2	20	26	71	15,108	0	0	0	0	0
Trip 3	0	0	0	0	1	1	827	40,000	0
Trip 4	8	11	92	13,678	2	2	12	20,000	0
Trip 5	0	0	0	0	0	0	0	0	16

Above we have five P&D trips, and as you can see, the workload for each trip is different. We're going to say that each driver drove 150 miles and worked 10.0 hours during the day. For example, Driver One picked up and delivered 21 shipments, 150 handling units (pieces), and had 30,000 pounds of LTL (a shipment less than 15,000 pounds) work on the truck in 12 stops. On the other hand, Driver Five picked and dropped 16 trailers at customer locations. You can see the diversity of the trips. If you were to measure the drivers by stops per hour, which driver has the best opportunity to be the most productive of the group? How about pounds per man-hour? Wages as a percent of revenue? That one has a lot to do with the type of freight and whether it is direct, or mixed with direct and partner freight, doesn't it? The picture gets kind of fuzzy, as you can see. Every shipment has a different cost. You really cannot tell how much capacity each run has or the true utilization solely based on 10 hours of work and 150 miles of driving. Are you beginning to see how difficult, if not impossible, it is to measure cost and capacity using traditional productivity methods that date back to the days of regulation?

The LTL Carrier Operates in a World of Constraints

We operate in a world of constraints. The constraints of a linehaul trailer are pretty easy. You can only scale so much weight and you only have a certain amount of cube to work with. In P&D, it's not that easy. To measure the capacity and cost relationship of a P&D run, the variables must be measured with respect to time. How many hours is the driver on the street? You must know the mileage and geography of the trip to determine the time it should take to complete the trip. Each shipment is different, so you must know the time it takes to load or unload each shipment at a customer's location based on making the stop, handling the paperwork, and handling the pieces or handling units of the shipment. What is the weight of the shipment? What is the density of the shipment? How long will it take to unload given the weight and density? A carrier must be able to determine the time requirement for all of the above variables to understand cost. If you cannot measure the time elements above, you will find yourself over-costing, under-costing, and occasionally, due to pure luck, costing a shipment correctly. Not very comforting, is it?

Oh, and the P&D trips above? As different as they are, they each require the same amount of work! Using engineered time allowances for each of the variables mentioned above, you will be able to measure the capacity and capacity utilization of each P&D run and with that capability, know your true cost. Having that capability sure does eliminate "management by thrashabout."

The ability to properly measure the capacity of a P&D operation also provides the ability to fairly set sales goals for the sales team. By determining the operational capacity of a terminal, real and measurable sales goals can be developed. This also gives the terminal and the company an understanding of how much additional business they can handle without adding any additional cost in the P&D, dock, and linehaul operations.

As we have noted several times in this book, the key to building long-term sustainable profitability is knowing how much operational capacity is available, growing the terminal and company, and absorbing new business with capacity already in place.

Don't throw more drivers, hours, overtime, trucks, trailers, and so on on at new business. Given today's driver shortage, having this information might make you feel more at ease. You may find you have more capacity than you thought you did, which should ease the level of driver pressure you thought you had.

Fallacies of Traditional Costing Systems in Costing Pickup & Delivery

In the example above, traditional costing results in over-costing pickup and delivery. Let's dive into this statement.

First, traditional systems assume the P&D operation is at 100% capacity. In my 33 years in the LTL industry, I have yet to see a P&D operation that did not have a minimum of 35% available capacity. Traditional cost models cannot measure capacity and capacity utilization, so they are not able to factor into the costing and pricing process the value of that excess capacity to the company. Simply put, you over-cost potential new business and cost yourself out of market share. Also, with traditional cost models, too much cost is assigned to current business and the carrier cannot accurately evaluate the value of a particular customer to the company.

Most traditional costing systems apply a stem-mile cost to every shipment. Again, you run the risk of applying too much cost in the process and costing yourself out of market share. A P&D run is already in a particular area, so calculate the cost of the trip and the incremental cost of picking up or delivering a shipment while in a particular area.

Let's begin our journey to understanding pickup and delivery cost, capacity, and productivity.

Consider the diagram below.

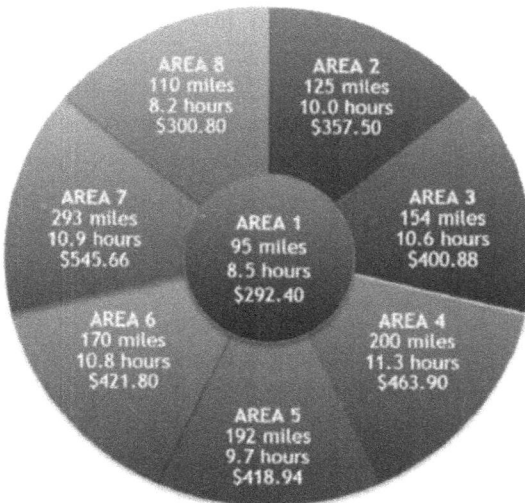

Since the operations department is responsible for 65 to 70 cents of each revenue dollar in costs, it makes sense to tie costing to the operations department instead of drawing costing factors from the income statement. There are a couple of reasons for this. First, the income statement is always in a state of flux because of adjustments, workdays in a month, and other factors. Second, the income statement assumes the pickup and delivery operation is operating at 100% capacity, which we know is not the case.

The first step in the process is to identify each terminal's operating area. Where do the P&D units operate on a daily basis? Divide up the terminal's operating area into cost areas that best reflect how the terminal puts their P&D fleet on the street each day.

The cost of operating in each area is different, as is the capacity available in each area. Notice Area 1 in the example above. They are averaging 95 miles per P&D trip and the drivers are on the street an average of 8.5 hours a day. Notice P&D Area 7. The drivers in Area 7 average 293 miles per trip and are on the street an average of 10.9 hours a day. That's a big difference. The cost for this carrier to run a P&D trip in Area 1 (based on the wage and fringe cost per hour for a driver and variable cost per mile) is $292.40, but in Area 7 the cost to run a trip averages $545.66. The capacity available from a work standpoint is different as well. A driver in Area 1 only drives 95 miles, so that driver has the capacity to do more work in a day than the driver who travels 293 miles. If a carrier cannot distinguish the difference, the carrier does not know its true operating cost and cannot accurately cost a shipment.

Look at the diagram once more. Traditional cost-based costing models develop terminal costs for the costing system based on averages of the terminal. If a carrier uses this methodology, the carrier will over-cost business in Area 1 and under-cost business in the outlying areas. In that case, where do you think the P&D operation is every day? Yep, out in the boondocks! I see this in *every* carrier I work with—without exception! The carrier wants the business in Area 1 and other low-cost operating areas, but using traditional methods costs the carrier out of those other segments of the market.

Updated methodology should be used for every terminal in the company. Each customer within the company should be assigned to a terminal and cost area within the terminal based on the zip code. The zip code is tied to an operating area within the terminal. So if a shipment is picked up from the Atlanta terminal P&D Area 1, and is to be delivered by the Richmond terminal P&D Area 4, the pickup cost is based on the cost of operating in Atlanta, P&D Area 1, and the delivery cost will be based on the cost of operating in Richmond, P&D Area 4.

Small Changes Produce Large Changes in Either the Up or Down Direction

Take a look at the P&D Detail report below. You will notice the terminal ran 168 P&D runs or trips for the week, or an average of 34 per day. Based on the engineered time allowances, they only had enough work for 137.60 P&D trips total, or 28 P&D trips a day. Under the "Performance" section, you will notice two headings: One is DVR for driver's performance, and the other MGT for management performance. The management performance number is 121.25. What this number tells management is that the P&D cost for that week was 21.25% higher than it should have been based on the work available to perform, miles driven, and hours used. The number also tells us this terminal has the capacity to do 21.25% more work with the cost already in place. There you have it: P&D capacity!

Let's crunch some numbers and see if we can validate that statement. In the example above, the carrier has a wage and fringe cost per hour of $30.22 for a P&D driver. The variable cost per mile for a P&D unit is $1.12.

If we take the net hours, or time on the street performing P&D work (1,420.33), and multiply that by $30.22 per hour, we find the labor cost for the P&D operation that week was $42,922. Next, we take the total miles (24,916) and multiply that by the cost per mile ($1.12) and find our variable mileage (equipment) cost was $27,906. If we add the two numbers together the P&D operation for the terminal below was $70,828 for the week. Pretty expensive, isn't it? The drivers are averaging 8.45 hours per P&D trip and 148 miles per trip. If we take the $70,828 and divide that by 168 P&D trips (a trip is a driver's workday) we find the average cost for a P&D trip is $421.60.

Let's calculate what the impact of 1 additional stop per trip would have on this terminal. On the report you will find a column labeled PRWK, which stands for Productive Work. As you see, the terminal had 530.63 hours of productive work. That number is derived from the engineered time allowances I developed for that terminal. If we take that number and divide it by the total number of trips (168) we find that drivers averaged 3.16 hours of productive work out of the 8.45 they were on the street. Now, we can take the total stops (2,110), add 94, and we see they made 2,204 stops that week picking up and delivering freight. That is an average of 13.12 stops per P&D trip.

If we take the total PRWK hours (530.63) based on the time allowances and divide that by 2,204 stops, we find that the average time per stop is .24 hours, or 14.4 minutes. If we add .24 hours of productive work to the average 3.16 PRWK hours per trip, one additional stop would increase PRWK per P&D trip from 3.16 to 3.40 hours. Now, let's take our total PRWK (530.63) and divide that by 3.40 hours of PRWK; we find that one additional stop per trip would reduce the P&D trips run from 168 to 156 for the week. So .24 hours or 14.4 minutes of additional PRWK (one stop) would reduce P&D trips by 12 for the week. The average cost of a P&D trip is $421.60. If we take $421.60 and multiply that by 12 (number of trips reduced) the terminal would save $5,059 dollars that week. Annualized, that one stop would save the terminal—and therefore the company—$263,078!

Small changes produce large changes in either the up of down direction.

Matching Sales with Operational Capacity

There is another, more positive way of looking at this available capacity in P&D. We are not here to put drivers out of work. Drivers are too hard to find and it's our responsibility as leaders to ensure they can provide for their families. They made a commitment to us when they came on board and they depend on us to know what the heck we're doing!

What we really want to do is grow our revenue base and absorb that additional revenue with capacity and cost already in place. That is how we build leverage and build long-term, sustainable profitability. We know our true operating cost because we can measure capacity and capacity utilization, and we are able to calculate the value of filling that excess capacity with new business. Unlike traditional costing systems that assume the carrier is operating at 100% capacity, the updated model I've presented will show that more market share is available because the carrier can factor in the value of excess capacity. It won't over-cost potential business.

Let's look at the P&D Summary Report below and crunch some more numbers.

As we know, this terminal has the capacity to perform 21.25% more work with the cost already in place. How can we approach this from a sales standpoint? Notice on the report that the terminal handled 3,170 LTL shipments. Let's use that number for our projection. If we take 3,170 and multiply that number by 1.2125 (our excess capacity, 21.25%) we get 3,844. That tells us the terminal has the capacity to handle 3,844 LTL shipments. If we subtract 3,170 from 3,844 we are left with 674. This terminal should be able to handle an additional 674 LTL shipments a week, based on these numbers. That's 135 shipments per day. If revenue per shipment is $125.00, we see that the terminal can handle an additional $16,874 in additional revenue each day without adding any additional P&D cost. How do you think that would impact profitability? Would you take half of that? Can you see this helping sales management in setting revenue goals?

Remember that "The Formula" is based on understanding capacity and capacity utilization so that as revenue growth occurs, the carrier absorbs that additional increase with capacity already in place. That reduces variable cost per shipment, increases contribution dollars per shipment, and life is good.

However, if a carrier cannot measure its capacity and capacity utilization, it will not know its real cost. I'm sure you'll agree that the traditional productivity measurements in use today by LTL carriers just do not have the capability to measure true cost, leaving carriers unable to factor in the value of unused capacity in operations from a pricing standpoint.

Build Operating Leverage through Pickup and Delivery

"The Formula" is all about growing your organization and absorbing the growth without adding additional capacity in the form of tractors, trucks, trailers, drivers, or hours. That's why knowing capacity, utilization of capacity, and excess capacity available is crucial. Remember that the local and regional carrier makes money in the P&D operation. A next-day or two-day carrier must run their line-haul trailers whether the trailer has 10 bills on it or 20 bills on it because of service commitments. Therefore, P&D is the leverage point for this type of carrier.

Study the table below. Once you understand it, you will have the picture and that "Aha" moment will hit you.

	Company A	Company B
Wage & Fringe - Cost per Hour	$ 25.06	$ 22.32
P&D - Cost per Mile	$ 1.0468	$ 0.9931
P&D - Hours per Trip	9.1	9.0
P&D - Miles per Trip	134	143
P&D - Cost per Trip	$ 368.31	$ 342.89
Productive Work Hours per Trip (Stops, shipments, handling units, weight)	4.22	3.70
Makeup of Productive Work per Trip		
Stops	16	11
Shipments	23	13
Handling Units	92	65
Weight	23,604	20,183
Average Cost to Pickup or Deliver a Shipment	$16.01	$ 26.37
OPERATING RATIO	91	100

Take two competing companies. Let's consider terminal A for one company and terminal B for the other company. These two terminals compete against each other every day. They are in the same city and mirror each other in terms of geographic territory.

Notice that Company A has a driver wage and fringe cost of $25.06, and Company B, $22.32. At first glance, one might believe Company A is the high-cost carrier when comparing the two. Also notice that Company A has a higher cost per mile than Company B. There is only 6 minutes of difference in time on the street, with Company A at 9.1 hours and Company B at 9.0 hours. Company A's miles per trip are 134 and Company B's, 143. When you look at the unit costs, Company A is also the high-cost carrier. Looking at cost per P&D Trip, Company A is the higher of the two at $368.31 and Company B lower at $342.89. Looking at these numbers alone, it appears that Company A has the higher cost of the two carriers.

Not true!

Notice the Productive Work Hours per Trip! Based on engineered time allowances, the drivers for Company A do 4.22 hours of productive work and Company B's drivers spend only 3.70 hours of their day performing productive work. Notice the difference in the makeup of each P&D trip. The bottom line is that Company A is the low-cost carrier, even though their cost per hour, cost per mile, and cost per P&D trip are significantly higher than Company B's. As you can see, just by using a simple average, we can determine that every shipment picked up or delivered costs $16.01 for Company A and $26.37 for Company B. Who is the low-cost carrier now?

Company A's operating ratio is 91, while Company B always wallows around breakeven. Company A has lower miles per P&D trip due to their level of productivity. They created their own freight density and therefore drive fewer miles between stops.

To properly cost P&D, a carrier must know the capacity available in P&D and also the capacity utilization. If you cannot measure those two elements, you do not know your P&D cost. We saw earlier how ineffective, inaccurate, and inconsistent using traditional productivity and cost measurements are. An LTL carrier operates in a world of constraints. In P&D those constraints include location, hours, miles, and type of freight. Those variables determine how much capacity and work a driver can perform. We'll delve into dock and linehaul trailer utilization next.

Summary:

Local and regional LTL carriers must understand how to leverage the pickup and delivery operation. The key to developing a successful P&D operation to build operating leverage into the company begins by knowing the capacity available in P&D, and the level of capacity utilization of the P&D operation. The next step is to get the inbound (morning) supervisors, city dispatchers, and outbound (evening) supervisors on the same page. The morning operation (inbound) can put a productive P&D operation on the street, but if the city dispatchers' objective is a "stress free" workday, they can turn what was a productive P&D operation into a very costly one in a hurry. I have a saying: "If your city dispatchers aren't sweating bullets, you're not making money from your P&D operation." City dispatch is the pivotal department! They not only control the level of P&D cost for the day, but they can also increase P&D cost for other terminals by not getting drivers back in in a timely manner so that the outbound shift can meet their outbound linehaul cut times.

I spend time with city dispatchers and I see two crucial errors of commission. First, they react to their day, and second, they create problems by giving drivers multiple pickups at one time, losing the driver! City dispatchers must be proactive.

When I was getting my commercial pilot's license I remember my flight instructor telling me that as pilot in command, you cannot sit in the cockpit flying along, enjoying the view. He told me that if I wasn't flying the airplane 25 miles ahead of my current position, I was behind the airplane. Those were *very* wise words. The same holds true for city dispatchers. Building a strong P&D operation requires everyone being on the same page, thinking ahead, and helping each other. It is a team effort. When I was coaching college football I learned very quickly that the player who is playing for his own stats is poison and will tear a team apart. That is absolutely terrifying for a coach! The same holds true for operations. Inbound, city dispatch, and outbound have to work together as a team, but more often than not, I see those three positions operating in silos.

P&D is THE critical function that determines the level of success in implementing "The Formula." Changing the culture of that operation is by far the largest obstacle in building operating leverage, which in turn creates the foundation for long-term sustainable profitability.

CHAPTER 5

Dock and Linehaul Trailer Utilization

"If you are not the market leader; that means competition has passed you...you have not been doing your homework."

—R. Sullivan

Everything we're discussing in the book is aimed at creating a blueprint to improve profitability. The foundation of improving profitability in an LTL carrier is the ability to measure capacity and capacity utilization in its pickup and delivery operation, linehaul operation, and dock operation so management can understand the carrier's true cost. A carrier's costing system must be able to determine the value of unused capacity in the costing process to build market share. Then operations must absorb the added business with capacity already in place. When you do that, you'll be taking money to the bank in wheelbarrows!

Dock and platform operations and linehaul trailer utilization are very interesting and have a huge impact on cost and service. Although dock labor cost (wages and fringes) averages 6 to 8% of each revenue dollar, the dock operation has a powerful effect on overall profitability.

If a dock is not properly staffed, linehaul trailers leave late, which makes arrivals late and, as you know, pressure on deliveries and pickups then increases, which in turn increases costs and jeopardizes service.

In my work with companies, I have seen the dock being micro-managed and improperly staffed based on volumes available at different segments of the day. When I ask management if they have run a queuing analysis I often get the deer-in-the-headlights look. We will return to queueing analysis later.

You read a book from beginning to end, but in business you begin at the end and work back to the beginning. Let's begin at the end to get to where we need to be.

Linehaul Trailer Utilization

Recall that an LTL carrier operates in a world of constraints. We thoroughly discussed the constraints in pickup and delivery in Chapter 4. In linehaul, constraints are different. A linehaul trailer only has a certain amount of space (cubic feet) available, and legal highway weight is a constraint. Another constraint in the linehaul operation is time and distance. I have engineered several scheduled linehaul systems over the years (not much fun to do, by the way!). A multiple-terminal operation must, like the airlines, have a scheduled system that puts the trailer at the destination terminal at a time that will allow service commitments to be made and P&D operating efficiencies and dock operating efficiencies to be achieved. On-time departure and arrival percentage must be higher than the airlines' percentage, though (I travel extensively, so please forgive this jab at the airlines.).

In many cases I have observed terminals putting the responsibility for service on linehaul. In a scheduled linehaul system, linehaul dispatchers are responsible for the timely movement of the trailer once it is turned over to them for dispatch. Similarly, airline operations has the responsibility of making sure the plane is at the gate on time so the people running the gate can get the plane loaded and turned around on time. The gate personnel see to it that passengers are queued up and ready to board the plane. In the same way, it is the responsibility of the terminal personnel to have the freight at the terminal ready to load on the trailer so linehaul dispatch can meet the scheduled departure time.

I have seen many cases in which terminals still have P&D units on the street picking up at 7 p.m. with freight on the truck that must meet a 7 p.m. departure deadline. If the terminal then expects linehaul to move the trailer to the destination terminal on time, that is just wrong! Terminals sometimes make sales commitments that they know are going to delay linehaul departures and expect the linehaul driver and department to magically get the trailer to the destination terminal on time.

A disciplined company holds the terminal responsible for making on-time cuts and not leaving any freight on the dock. Follow the principle of starting with the end: What are the linehaul cut times (the end)? Given those cut times, what time does the terminal need to have freight at the terminal queued up to load? The terminal should take this information into account when managing its P&D operation that is on the street (the beginning).

As I wrote earlier, local or regional carriers make money in pickup and delivery operation, and they have almost complete control over that operation. The linehaul methodology given below is critical for local and regional carriers because linehaul trailers must be run whether the trailer has 5 shipments or 25 shipments, since local and regional carriers are more than likely next-day service providers and must run the trailers to make service. In other words, these carriers do not have as much control over linehaul as they do over pickup and delivery and dock. With that in mind, let's move on to linehaul measurements.

Linehaul Measurements

As is the case with pickup and delivery measurements, traditional linehaul measurements can be misleading. Of course the mainstay measurement of linehaul is load average, but load average is only one number a carrier should be concerned with. To determine if a linehaul operation is productive and efficient, we must look at several numbers and the trend in their direction.

Let's look at load average for the three different companies below.

Load Average (pounds)
Company 1	24,675
Company 2	22,091
Company 3	24,839

If you just looked at load average, you would pick Company 3 as the most efficient of the companies, with a load average of 24,839 pounds. But let's add another number to the mix, weight per shipment in linehaul.

Weight Per Shipment
Company 1	1,508
Company 2	1,175
Company 3	1,647

Does that get you thinking a little differently about which carrier might be the most efficient? Load average has a lot to do with the type of freight. Let's throw another number into the mix to see if that impacts load average: bills per linehaul trailer.

Bills per Linehaul Trailer
Company 1	16.6
Company 2	18.9
Company 3	15.4

Are you beginning to change your mind about load average as a measurement of utilization or efficiency? I would say that even though Company 2 has the lowest load average, driven by weight per shipment, they have the most efficient linehaul utilization when measured by bills per trailer. Now, freight density (pounds per cubic feet) can have some impact on efficiency, but I have found this methodology very sound.

I remember sitting in a meeting several years ago with a regional vice president conducting a performance review with one of his terminal managers. He was all over the manager because the manager's terminal load average was dropping. While he was tearing this poor terminal manager up about his load average, I was quietly making the calculations above. After the VP finished with the manager, I showed the VP my calculations. The terminal's weight per shipment in linehaul had dropped 74 pounds due to a large national account coming on board with a huge number of minimum shipments. His bills per trailer had actually increased by 3.2 bills.

I will give the VP credit: He called the manager back in and corrected his mistake. That was a class act on his part. After that, the company began looking at several measurements to determine efficiency, such as bills per trailer, miles per bill, and weight per bill. It was a good example of why carriers should be wary of using traditional measurements to determine performance.

Empty Trailers

Remember one of the most important points in this book: If a carrier cannot measure capacity and capacity utilization, the carrier does not know its cost. We have explored that principle in pickup and delivery; now let's look at linehaul cost.

As you know, a linehaul trailer has two primary constraints: weight and cubic feet (cube). You can only legally scale so much weight and you only have a certain number of cubic feet to work with in a trailer. It is easy to identify trailers that are empty; there's no freight on them. However, I have seen many trailers dispatched with only 2,000, 3,000, 5,000, or 7,000 pounds. Not empty, are they? In the old days terminal managers would put three or four shipments on a trailer and give it to linehaul to move. Didn't have to report that as an empty, did they? Hey, I managed terminals for years, so I know all the tricks to mask poor productivity in P&D, linehaul, and dock!

A company must be able to measure equivalent empty trailers in linehaul. The utilization of a linehaul trailer must be determined by weight or cube; use the higher of the two numbers to determine utilization. By doing this, unused available linear feet can be determined, and based on the size of the trailer you can then determine what is called "equivalent empty trailers." Let's revisit our three companies and see where they are. Here is one month of data.

	Empty Trailers	Equivalent Empty Trailers
Company 1	0	103.55
Company 2	30	377.51
Company 3	11	125.56

These numbers show a different picture. Just as management measures capacity and capacity utilization in P&D using engineered time allowances, hours, geographic location, and miles (constraints in P&D), determining linehaul trailer utilization based on weight or cube to calculate equivalent empty trailers measures capacity in linehaul. In the above example, all three companies have a tremendous amount of excess capacity in linehaul. This information should also be lane-specific so linehaul lane balance factors can be calculated for costing.

Lane Balance Factors

Another key number that must be calculated is lane balance factors. Using the TPG methodology, lane imbalances can be calculated, entered into the lane file for each pair of terminals, and used in calculating linehaul cost for each shipment. Again, you must have lane-specific information (like the information above for the three companies) on a terminal-by-terminal basis and lane-direction basis. If you cannot accomplish this, you are under-costing linehaul in some directions and over-costing linehaul in other directions. Lane balance factors are crucial for properly costing linehaul.

Let's take a look at some factors.

⟶	HUD	SUP	STC	FAR	TRI	LAX
HUD	-	1.50	1.29	0.99	1.50	1.54
SUP	0.50	-	0.29	0.40	0.94	0.54
STC	0.71	1.71	-	0.70	1.65	1.25
FAR	1.01	1.60	1.30	-	1.50	1.55
TRI	0.50	0.86	0.35	0.50	-	0.60
LAX	0.46	1.46	0.75	0.45	1.40	-

Based on data from the TPG Trailer Utilization report, we can create lane balance factors. As you can see, from terminal HUD to terminal STC, the lane balance factor is 1.29. Notice that from STC to HUD, the factor is .71 and the two together add up to 2 (round trip). These factors are entered into the TPG lane file for the costing system. LTL carriers build the imbalance into the headhaul lane, and in this example HUD to STC is the headhaul lane. There is more freight going from HUD to STC than the opposite indirection, so you build that imbalance in that direction. This means linehaul cost for shipments traveling from HUD to STC will increase by 29% to cover the building imbalance. However, we need to move freight from STC to HUD, so we will reduce linehaul cost on those shipments by 29% to build the lane. If you don't use this methodology, you will under-cost business from HUD to STC. The imbalance will worsen and so will cost because trailers moved will increase over time.

It is critical for a local or regional carrier to have the above information for proper utilization measurement, and to be able to calculate lane balance factors for each lane in order to cost linehaul properly. If you do not know your capacity and capacity utilization, you do not know your cost!

Dock Operations

Dock Philosophy

The efficiency and organization of dock operations have a huge impact on service and cost in pickup and delivery and linehaul. As I mentioned earlier in the chapter, dock cost (wages and fringes) runs about 6 to 8% of each revenue dollar. A short-haul regional carrier will see linehaul cost as a percent of revenue in the 19- to 22%-range. Pickup and delivery will run between 32 and 38% of each revenue dollar. This includes drivers' wage and fringe cost per hour and variable cost per mile for equipment.

Based on the numbers above, approximately 57% of each revenue dollar will be consumed by linehaul cost and P&D cost. Pretty interesting statistic that makes you think twice about P&D, isn't it? This figure is why I keep saying that local or regional carriers make money in P&D. Long-haul carriers leave millions of dollars on the table each year because they focus primarily on linehaul due to their length of haul. P&D is a *huge* missed opportunity for long-haul carriers.

Docks have a tendency to be micromanaged because, unlike P&D, management is right there with the dockworkers and has more control. This is different from P&D, where drivers are pretty much on their own once they leave the terminal. My philosophy is: Have enough help on the dock to put an efficient pickup and delivery operation on the street each day and a well utilized linehaul operation out each night. Meet scheduled cut times because missed cut times have a ripple effect on service and P&D cost. My engineered standards for the dock operation are developed based on this philosophy.

Here's an interesting story. Several years ago, an engineering school wanted to validate the engineered standards I developed. They immersed themselves in a carrier that uses my system. They rode with P&D drivers, worked the dock, and got their hands dirty. They reported my pickup and delivery standards were fair and attainable, but my dock standards were a little loose. Once I explained my philosophy to them, they replied that it made perfect sense.

Dock efficiency and dock organization is critical for efficient pickup and delivery operation and linehaul trailer utilization.

Dock Methodology

Let me reiterate that traditional dock productivity measurements that date back to the days of regulation days are inaccurate and misleading, and should not be in use today. Many carriers use these outdated measurements, which include bills per hour, pounds per man-hour, wages as a percent of revenue, and other measurements that give you "in the mix" numbers overall. But shipments are different. They have different handling units (pieces), weight is different, the density (PCF) of shipments is different, and each shipment requires its own time to crossdock.

Also, when carriers use cost data based on traditional productivity measurements, they both over-cost shipments and under-cost shipments and hope it works out. Each terminal's dock is different, and the freight moving through terminals can certainly be different. All of those differences must be measured.

Believe me, using averages to measure productivity and cost is like playing Russian roulette—you better know what you're doing, just as in P&D. I have seen terminals with four doors and a dock that is 60 feet long and 40 feet wide. I have also seen terminals that are huge breakbulks as well as having a local operation that has 200 doors and a 1,000-foot-long dock that is 110 feet wide.

A shipment that weighs 1,000 pounds with a density of 10 PCF and 5 handling units will cost quite a bit more if it goes through a terminal with a dock that's 1,000 feet long and 110 feet wide than if it goes through a terminal with a 60-foot-long dock that's 40 feet wide.

Another factor in properly measuring productivity and cost is the freight mix moving through a terminal. A terminal that handles a lot of heavy industrial freight is different from a terminal that handles mostly distribution or retail freight.

There are many variables that must be accounted for to properly measure dock productivity and cost for each shipment. Engineered time allowances for the shipment, handling units, and weight adjusted for density are essential to properly measure dock productivity and cost for a shipment.

Engineered Time Allowances and Methodology

A dock may have several different operations within the terminal. There is the inbound operation, outbound operation, and perhaps an intermediate (breakbulk/relay) operation. A dock may have shipments that require an appointment, distribution, or sort-and-segment freight. Dock operations may also have partners, or interline, or customers that bring the freight to the dock and unload the freight.

Given these many possible operations, standards must take into consideration the methodology or handling characteristics of each segment. For example, a certain percentage of inbound freight will go from linehaul trailer to the dock, will be set down, and will be handled again later to properly load a P&D unit. Outbound freight should go from the P&D unit directly to the linehaul trailer. It should not be handled again. The same should hold true for intermediate terminal freight.

There is additional cost involved in handling appointment freight on a dock. I have found appointment shipments are not crossdocked, but touched or moved an additional 4.6 times before being put out for delivery. Another example is sort-and-seg. A fully loaded trailer may be dropped at a dock, and the terminal then has to sort out and build the shipments, shrink-wrapped on a skid, and create the paperwork that follows the shipment. That requires more time to handle than a traditional outbound shipment that goes from truck to truck.

If a costing system cannot differentiate the time and cost for each shipment based on the category the shipment falls into, the carrier is costing "in the mix" again, and once more, that dog ain't gonna hunt!

Dock Capacity

If a carrier's dock productivity system does not use time allowances for different categories, management does not know its dock cost and is not costing shipments accurately. The dock system should be able to calculate the hours allowed for each of those categories based on the shipments crossdocked, and the terminal should measure the allowed hours, based on time allowances, against hours actually used to calculate dock throughput capacity. For example, if the system allows a terminal 400 hours for the dock operation and the terminal uses 480 hours, the dock has the capacity to handle 17% more freight than is currently being handled.

We have been saying from the beginning that the key to profitability is knowing the capacity the company has in pickup and delivery, linehaul, and dock, and the percent of capacity utilization. Then sales finds opportunities for additional business, the pricing department determines whether or not the new business is good for the company, and if the business is brought onboard, the operations department absorbs that new business with capacity and variable cost already in place! Don't you just love it when a plan comes together?

Summary Operations:
Pickup and Delivery, Dock, and Linehaul Trailer Utilization

As we have determined, an LTL carrier is extremely capital intense. That intensity is driven by the capacity built into the company to handle customers' freight in pickup and delivery, dock, and linehaul trailer utilization. If management does not know its capacity and percent of utilization, they are gambling that it all works out in the end.

Variable cost as a percent of each revenue dollar is the key number that drives profitability for the LTL carrier. The level of variable cost determines the level of contribution left over to cover fixed cost and overhead and add to profitability. The operating efficiency and productivity and utilization of the operations department determines the level of variable cost in the company. A costing system must be able to accurately measure the time it takes to handle a shipment in pickup and delivery and dock, and measure space from a weight or cube standpoint in linehaul. The constraints in the operations world determine those factors for costing.

I work with companies that have all the latest and greatest technology. They have the inbound planning systems, GPS mapping, dispatch systems, and administrative software that can make a company paperless. All of that is great and much needed and I recommend many of those products to my clients. However, I have worked with companies that have all that wonderful and dandy technology and they still lose money.

Thanks to 29 years in the trenches, I can confidently tell you why that is. Recall that in Chapter 1 I wrote that the major issue in LTL carrier management is not that leaders cannot solve their problems, but that they cannot see their problems because they use outdated, ineffective productivity measurements that are "in the mix" and based on averages that do not measure capacity and capacity utilization. Therefore leaders cannot effectively manage the variable cost of the company, which drives profitability.

Our industry is not as strong as it could be from the standpoint of profitability and return on investment. Even with all the latest and best technology, most carriers spend each day banging their heads against the barrier of complexity because they cannot see, and therefore cannot measure, the constraints they operate with each day. Because of the outdated productivity and cost measurements in use, they go through each day managing by thrashabout. Most companies have no idea how much operational capacity they have in each terminal and the company as a whole, and so they cannot measure their percent of utilization. Therefore the carrier has little idea of the potential value to the company of the unused capacity in operations from a sales standpoint. When the costing system and methodology in use assumes the company is operating at 100% capacity, which all other systems do, it becomes a vicious cycle the carrier can't break. As a result, profitability and return on investment are not maximized.

In any sport, in any company, fundamentals are enduring. As I wrote earlier in this book, a championship football coach told over 1,000 coaches at a convention that even with all the schemes, looks, and reads teams go through to confuse their opponents, the team that blocks the best and tackles the best on Saturday afternoon will probably win the game. As leaders in operations we need to understand the fundamentals better than our competition. I'm not talking about the fundamentals of getting a shipment from one terminal to the next—heck, that's easy! I'm talking about the fundamentals of understanding cost, capacity, capacity utilization, and constraints at a level where we can operate more efficiently, productively, and control profitability by understanding variable cost and how to manage it. Understand the game being played. Fundamentals are enduring!

My dream is to one day create a college-level course or create a school that teaches nothing but LTL profitability. My absolute passion is teaching and coaching leaders at all levels in a carrier how to better understand the fundamentals of cost and profitability that relate to their companies.

Let's move on and look at the importance of understanding both your customer base and customer base analysis.

CHAPTER 6:

You Have to Know
What's Going on with Your Customer Base

"It's very simple! You find the customers that are killing you; the ones that are sucking cash out of the company and you either get a price increase or you fire them! It's that simple!"

—R. Sullivan

I have been looking forward to sharing this chapter's insights with you very much. As I have noted often in this book, a leader must continue to learn and grow in order to continue to achieve.

This chapter is based on a real-life client experience.

The First Step:
Your customer base can tell you a lot about your company

Understanding what business fits your operating characteristics and cost structure is essential. As said several times before, you can't be all things to all people. The first step is to break your customer base down into weight breaks. However make certain you have the customer files properly setup with correct density and special handling. An example of special handling would be an operation where the carrier drops a trailer at a customer's dock and the customer loads the shipments on the trailer. The cost to drop or pick a trailer is different than a live load or unload. Obviously a live pick up is where the driver stays with the trailer and physically loads the shipments on the trailer. Another example of special handling would be a customer that brings a trailer containing freight to the carrier and drops the trailer for the carrier to unload. In this case the carrier would not have a pickup cost for those shipments. So, the first step is to make certain you're applying the correct density or dim weight and special handling.

In the example below (an actual carrier's customer base) we can look at the numbers and figure out what better fits our operation and cost structure. This in turn allows the carrier to provide direction to the sales department and gives the pricing department data to make better pricing decisions.

First of all it is important to understand this is an LTL carrier with the cost structure of an LTL carrier, which is totally different than that of a TL (Truckload carrier). Through my years I have learned Truckload shipments to do not mix well with LTL because the cost structures are so different.

Weight Breaks	Shipments	Revenue	Variable Cost	Contr Dollars	Contr Ratio	Var Cost % Revenue	Revenue Per Ship	Var Cost Per Ship	Contr Shipment
1 - 500	10,650	$ 708,643	$ 330,926	$ 377,718	214.14	46.70	$ 66.54	$ 31.07	$ 35.47
500 - 999	5,787	469,438	225,572	243,867	208.11	48.05	81.12	38.98	$ 42.14
1000 - 1499	3,124	318,820	152,569	166,251	208.97	47.85	102.06	48.84	$ 53.22
1500 - 1799	1,383	167,598	79,049	88,549	212.02	47.17	121.18	57.16	$ 64.03
1800 - 1999	813	102,138	50,645	51,493	201.68	49.58	125.63	62.29	$ 63.34
2000 - 3999	4,364	717,651	342,101	375,550	209.78	47.67	164.45	78.39	$ 86.06
4000 - 6999	2,625	725,327	330,394	394,932	219.53	45.55	276.31	125.86	$150.45
7000 - 9999	646	234,030	118,516	115,514	197.47	50.64	362.28	183.46	$178.81
10000 - 13999	312	112,606	70,380	52,226	174.21	62.50	360.92	225.58	$167.39
14000 - 15000	54	23,739	15,372	8,368	154.44	64.75	439.62	284.66	$154.96
> 15000	288	178,423	128,971	49,452	138.34	72.28	619.52	447.82	$171.71
What if									
1 - 3,999	26,121	$ 2,484,289	$ 1,180,862	1,303,427	210.38	47.53%			$ 49.90
15 Shipments Run LTL Average for May	15	$ 95.11	$ 45.21	49.90					$748.49

The numbers you see above were run through the cost model and operating inefficiencies have been removed so we could get a true picture of the quality of business. Remember, a carrier's operating inefficiencies belong to the carrier, not the customer.

What we're looking for is the point where variable cost as a percent of revenue goes upside down. For this carrier that point is the 7,000 – 9,999 point. At that point variable costs exceeds the variable cost percent of the carrier. Even though contribution dollars per shipment is greater, the capacity in terms of cube and / or weight shrinks and the carrier's total contribution dollars will drop. Not contribution dollars per shipment, but total contribution dollars because the larger shipments take up more capacity, which means less shipments per trailer or P&D run. Also we found that the larger volume shipments took longer to pick up or deliver diminishing the ability to build operating leverage and they added tremendous complexity to the operation. Another, crucial finding was the volume shipments reduced pickup capacity and the carrier kept adding drivers so they could make their LTL pickups.

At the bottom of the spreadsheet you see a cell with "What if" typed in it. We determined our sweet spot is 1 to 3,999. If priced correctly we will look at 4,000 – 6,999. The pure LTL peddle runs are averaging 15 LTL shipments. As you can see in the 1 – 3,999 range the average contribution dollars per shipments is $49.90. With that level of contribution per shipment and 15 shipments the average contribution dollars per pickup and delivery run would be around $748.49. The peddle runs that had volume shipments, above the 7,000 pound mark were less productive and averaged around in the $550.00 range in contribution dollars per peddle run.

The carrier immediately began training the account reps and the people who did spot quotes on what to target. They would still entertain volume shipments, but those had to go through the pricing department for approval.

Once you understand what your customer base is telling you, the next step is to create "The Bucket List".

The Scenario

A company signed me to help them get back on track. The company was stagnant from a growth standpoint and had incurred two years of deep losses. The balance sheet was becoming waterlogged and the banks were circling. Though the company's leaders were good people and good leaders, they just didn't know what to do to get things back on track.

My modus operandi when working with a company was to first install my costing system and begin feverishly working on building operating efficiencies to turn the company around. Now, for all you "truckers" like me: This company had an operating ratio of 116.8. Not pretty, right?

I began my analysis of the pickup and delivery, dock, and linehaul operations, thinking that I would put together a plan to drive out enough operating inefficiencies to get the company back to profitability and I would be a hero.

Wrong! Once I got into the numbers, I realized that even if I got them to 100% efficiency in P&D, dock, and linehaul trailer utilization, they would still be at a 106 operating ratio. Given prepaid items, depreciation, and non-cash accounts, they would still be a little shy of cash breakeven! As we all know, cash is king. If you can't get to and maintain a cash-positive position, you're not going have much fun or sleep well.

I had some sleepless nights as I tried to come up with a tool or process that would allow us to see a complete picture. We did know our operating inefficiencies and we could cost potential business brought to us by the sales team.

The Bucket List

My brain was working overtime. As I thought through our situation, I concluded that every company has customers that are profitable, some that contribute but are not profitable, and some that do not even cover their variable or out-of-pocket costs. In the middle of the night, I suddenly woke up with the solution. I thought if we could segment our customer base into three "buckets," we might find our problem. I immediately called the head of IT and went through the concept. As a result, we created our Customer Base Analysis program, which provided the capability to determine the quality of our customer base.

Please take a look at the diagram below.

Transportation
Profitability Group

Customer-base segmentation...a must in our industry.

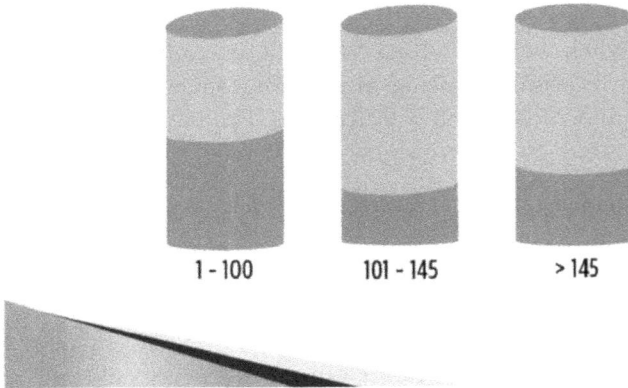

| 1 - 100 | 101 - 145 | > 145 |

Companies that cannot segment their customer base are missing opportunities to improve their profitability. Companies often focus on the profitability of accounts in their decision-making process with respect to divestment and retention of customers, but that is flawed thinking. In the example above, the breakeven contribution ratio is 145. This means that once variable cost is covered, the company needs a contribution rate of 45% above the variable cost level to cover fixed cost and overhead.

The customers in the first container, the 1–100 group, are not even covering variable cost. They have no value to the company. Also, when factoring in the timing of cash flow, those costs are paid out long before the company sees the cash in as a receivable, so these customers actually negatively affect cash flow as well as profitability.

The second group of customers is covering variable costs and providing some level of contribution to cover fixed costs and overhead, but these customers are not profitable. For example, if we had a customer with a 135 contribution ratio, that customer is covering variable costs and has a contribution rate of 35% to cover fixed cost and overhead. The operating ratio for that customer is 111.5. Using traditional thinking, many companies would cut that customer off if they could not get a substantial rate increase. This is where losses deepen in declining and failing carriers.

If the company cuts that customer, it simply makes matters worse, unless it can take enough cost out to neutralize the loss of contribution dollars. Most people think in terms of reducing P&D costs and/or dock costs, but it's not enough to consider those costs. To avoid making the situation worse, the company would not only have to cut enough variable or direct costs, but also have to cut costs that represent the loss of contribution dollars. Most carriers do not understand this concept and do not have a system that gives them the capability to analyze their costs and customer base at that level.

The third bucket contains the customers that are profitable. Your mission here is pretty simple: protect them with all your might!

By building what I call a "Bucket List" of the customers in those three buckets, you are well on your way to improving the productivity of your customer base.

What I Found in My Analysis

I knew my key number was contribution dollars per shipment, a number that is controlled by the relationship of variable cost to revenue. Revenue per shipment minus variable cost per shipment gives the contribution dollars per shipment. The higher that number is, the fewer shipments are needed to cover fixed cost, semi-fixed cost, and overhead. The lower that number, the higher the shipment count needed to cover fixed cost, semi-fixed, cost and overhead.

Transportation
Profitability Group

Customer-base segmentation...a must in our industry.

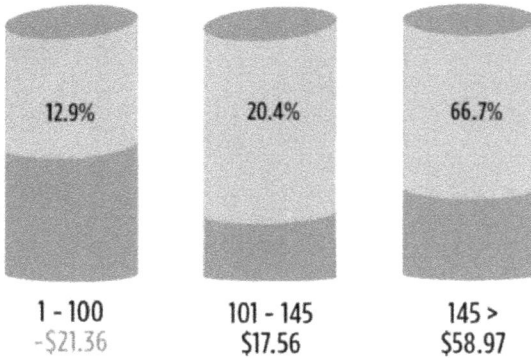

12.9%	20.4%	66.7%
1 - 100	101 - 145	145 >
-$21.36	$17.56	$58.97

Notice below that the 1-100 container is 12.9% of total shipment count and shows negative contribution dollars per shipment of ($21.36). Remember, the 1-100 container is variable cost. If a shipment has a contribution ratio of 90, the shipment is only covering 90% of variable cost. The more this container grows, the lower the overall contribution dollars per shipment.

The middle container (101 – 145) contains those shipments and customers that are not profitable, but are providing contribution dollars to help cover fixed cost and overhead. That container represents 20.4 % of total business. As you see from the illustration, the contribution dollars per shipment figure in the container averages a positive $17.56. Not the greatest, but not the worst.

The customers in the container in the >145 range are profitable and the company should do everything possible to keep those customers. That container represents 66.71% of total shipment count and shows positive contribution dollars per shipment of $58.97.

At this point, I understood the makeup of the customer base, but didn't quite know how to deal with it or what to do with it.

Transportation
Profitability Group

Traditional thinking can lead to SERIOUS trouble.

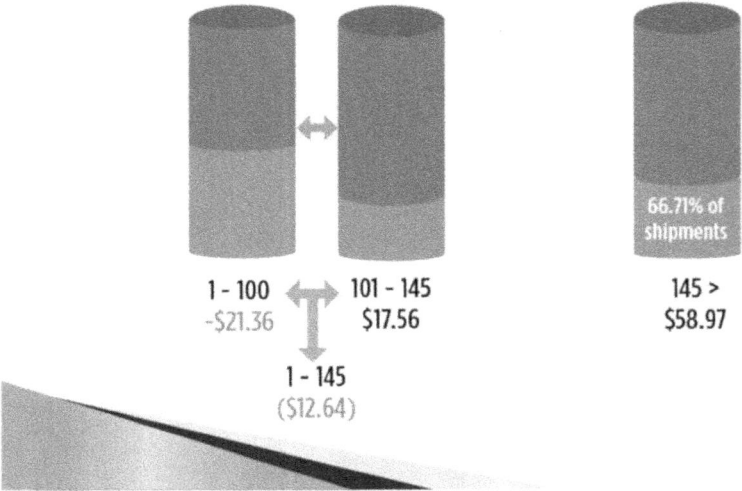

| 1 - 100 | 101 - 145 | 145 > |
| -$21.36 | $17.56 | $58.97 |

1 - 145
($12.64)

66.71% of shipments

The Ah-ha Moment

I decided to combine the 1–100 container and the 101–145 container to see the negative impact the 1–100 container had on the 101–145. As you can see below, the 1–100 container was so bad that when I put the two together we had a negative ($12.64) contribution dollars per shipment figure. The profitable container (66.71% of our shipments) was in effect trying both to neutralize the negative impact of the 1–100 container and to cover fixed cost and overhead and add profitability to the company.

We now knew what we had to do.

1. Improve the quality of our customer base by cleaning up the 1–100 container and obtaining rate increases for the customers in the 101–145 container.

2. Create a "don't-go-below contribution ratio" for new business. (Pricing is the number-one problem in underperforming companies.)

3. Hold the operations department accountable for improving operating efficiencies and maintaining service levels as sales and pricing managed the improvement of the customer base.

Transportation Profitability Group

Customer-base segmentation...a must in our industry.

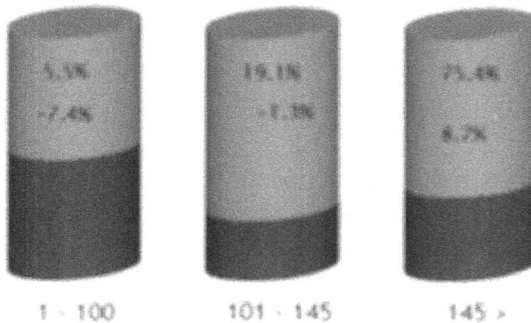

It Worked

As you can see below, the strategy worked. Notice the 1-100 container dropped from 12.9% to 5.5% of total shipment count, a 7.4% improvement. The 101-145 container actually declined 1.3%, due to more stringent pricing guidelines and rate increases in the 101-145 category that pushed some from the middle container to the profitable container.

The key figure, as you can see, is that the profitable container improved from 66.71% to 75.4% of total shipment count. That is a huge positive change.

Quality of revenue and quantity of revenue improved, due to the sales department's success in getting rate increases as well as generating an increase in overall revenue growth.

The other key piece that really made this strategy work was the COO of the company. If I had to take a hill in battle, I would want him with me. The company president supported the COO, and the COO really drove his terminal managers, who in turn drove their supervisors and employees to improve operating efficiencies in pickup and delivery, dock and platform, and linehaul trailer utilization.

Don't you just love it when a plan comes together?

Important Points to Remember:

Minimum shipments can be profitable, but they can be deadly. A carrier must really understand minimum shipments and their impact on profitability. Here is a minimum shipment example:

Shipment Revenue:	$65.00
Shipment Variable Cost:	$41.94
Contribution Dollars:	$23.06

For the carrier used in the illustrations above, this shipment has an operating ratio of 94. However, notice the contribution dollars per shipment figure is $23.06. This carrier's average contribution dollars per shipment is $39.25. As they handle more minimum shipments, the overall contribution per shipment will decline. Recall our earlier discussion about cost, volume, and contribution.

This example assumes one minimum shipment is being picked up and delivered. If you get multiple minimums at a stop, that's a different story. If you can drop a trailer and the shipper loads 30 or 40 minimum shipments onto the trailer, life is good!

On the flip side, if a customer's business is run through the costing model and it doesn't make the cut from a profitability standpoint, but the carrier will get $55.00 contribution per shipment from it, I might suggest they consider taking on the customer. If the carrier has excess capacity in linehaul and pickup and delivery and I am confident its culture in operations can absorb additional business with capacity already in place, I might suggest bringing that customer onboard and taking a look at it 90 days from that point.

Pricing is both an art and a science. Once more, you see why it is so important to understand the business you're in. You have to know your costs, and if you cannot measure capacity and capacity utilization, you really don't know your cost. It becomes a vicious cycle.

Account representatives send in pricing requests for new business to the pricing department, but in many cases the information is incomplete or inaccurate; the pricing department might or might not approve the pricing. It's kind of like flipping a coin. In many cases the pricing department will just deny the request due to incomplete information.

If you find yourself in this scenario, I would suggest another option. If you analyze the opportunity as carefully as possible and it appears to be "on the bubble" from a gut and data standpoint, perhaps you should bring the business on board.

However, the key to this process is to put the pricing in a tickler file to take a look at in 60 or 90 days, after you have some real-world experience handling the business. Once you have handled the business and can cost it properly, you will be able to make a better decision. You might decide that the business is okay and you can continue to handle, or it's not good and you can determine what needs to happen to make it a good account, or it's ugly, and you have to dump it.

At least you've given it a try. Now, I am not saying carriers should do this with every pricing request that comes through the door, but instead just the ones that through costing and gut seem to fit the company's needs. I tell my clients it is much more important to analyze an account after you have some experience with a customer because the information received on the front end (from the account representative and customer) is often inaccurate.

Summary

Understanding your customer base is a must for every company. If your costing process cannot remove non-related variable costs and operating inefficiencies from the costing process, you cannot judge the value of a customer to the company. If your costing system cannot measure capacity and capacity utilization you do not know your costs and cannot properly evaluate the productivity of a customer to the company. Over the years I have witnessed many carriers remove customers from their company based on direct costs or operating ratio, which makes things even worse. It's like hoping to extinguish a fire by pouring gasoline on it.

When you begin tinkering with your customer base and revenue, you had better know what you're doing because that is a *very* dangerous game.

CHAPTER 7

Getting Everyone on the Same Page: Performance-based Incentive Compensation

You must learn how to hold a team together. You must lift some men up, calm others down, until finally you've got one heartbeat. Then you've got yourself a team.

—Coach Bear Bryant

When I begin working with new carriers, I find many of them are still operating with a silo methodology. We see sales doing their thing, operations doing their thing, pricing and traffic doing their thing. In some cases, each department has its own goals and objectives that will move the company in the direction of improved performance and profitability, but usually the departments are loosely tied together. In some cases, they do not have goals and objectives. Sales hunts revenue and pricing maintains its standards, but the two do not have a formal game plan. Operations focuses on service and grunts a lot at the type of freight being brought onboard and the constraints sales and pricing puts on them due to customer requirements. Yet not often enough do these three key departments formally address those constraints.

In many companies, senior management approaches this dilemma with something called bonuses or incentive compensation to encourage everyone to work together for the common good. While admirable and a step in the right direction, traditional incentive programs have flaws.

1. They are generally "all-or-nothing" programs. If the goal or benchmark is not achieved, there is no payout. If the participants see the goal or benchmark is not going to be achieved, motivation wanes.

2. Underperforming departments are treated the same as departments that are performing exceptionally. For example, sales may be hitting its revenue goal, but operations is driving costs up, negatively impacting the success of all other participants, including sales.

There are other flaws, but those are the two major problems that render traditional bonus programs incapable of getting all departments on the same page.

Overview of a Successful Incentive Program

An incentive program should not be an all-or-nothing program. It should be designed to get every employee and every department on the same page, focused on the areas they have control over that will drive the company forward.

The goals people are held accountable for should involve only areas that the participant has control over. For example, an inbound supervisor should not be held accountable for ROI. Does the inbound supervisor's performance impact that number? Of course! However, inbound supervisors have control over and directly impact the success of P&D and dock performance, on-time performance, and claims, to suggest a few specific areas. If they are successful in improving performance in those areas, ROI should improve—if other departments within the company perform at the requisite levels. However, if inbound supervisors improve in their area, they should not be punished if another department (or departments) fails to perform.

Furthermore, the inbound supervisor's performance should not be an all-or-nothing situation. If part of the supervisor's compensation is based on service performance, the supervisor's performance-based compensation should rest on a sliding scale with two benchmarks, perfect and acceptable, allowing the supervisor the opportunity to receive some compensation as long as the number is between those levels. Perhaps the ultimate goal is 99% on-time delivery performance. In real life, there are areas that drive on-time performance that the inbound supervisor has little or no control over, such as on-time linehaul arrivals. If the linehaul trailer arrives two hours late, does that impact on-time performance? Absolutely—as well as P&D cost. Given factors like this, the inbound supervisor's on-time performance range might be from 95% to 99%, with a percentage of incentive-based earnings tied to each point within the range. This keeps the supervisor motivated to improve, rather than setting the bar at perfection, in which case the supervisor might near the end of the bonus period, see that his or her service is 97%, realize no bonus is possible, and stop trying to improve.

Tie the employee's bonus to the areas the employee has control over! Keep them motivated by giving them the opportunity to get a win if they continue to strive for excellence.

Where Do You Begin?

As you know, a company must not only be profitable, but also profitable enough to re-capitalize at a level that enables the company to be competitive in the markets served. So the program rules (to follow later in this chapter) should clearly state that the program will not kick in until the company hits a 96 operating ratio (this varies from company to company). Once the company hits a 96 operating ratio, senior management decides what percentage of the profit is going to be put in the "payout bucket." I have seen this range from 6% and up; this figure depends on how much of the profit senior management feels they can share. It's a subjective decision, but the figure should be meaningful enough to keep employees motivated to achieve goals.

The company should have a profitability goal for the year. In this example, let's use a 94 operating ratio. The incentive kicks in at a 96, but the annual goal is a 94.

Payout Rules

The payout can be monthly or quarterly. I would not recommend extending beyond one of those time frames because the closer you reward the employee to the goals achieved, the more motivated to continue achieving the person remains.

The company should pay a percentage of the incentive earned and hold a percentage back. If the employee earns $250.00, the company will only cut them a check for 85% of the incentive earned. The remaining 15% is put into another "bucket." If, at the end of the year, the company achieves the 94 operating ratio goal, the remaining 15% will be distributed to the employees. Let's suppose the company ended up with a 94.4 operating ratio and not the 94. The company will take the dollars in the 15% bucket and use those dollars to move the company to the 94 operating ratio. If any money is left over after achieving the 94 operating ratio, it is then distributed to the participants. It is also permitted for the company to pay interest into the 15% bucket for use of the employees' money during the year.

Another powerful approach is the tiered approach. The company might have a 94 operating ratio as the goal, but also have a 93 operating ratio as a stretch goal. If the 93 is reached, the company will distribute a higher level of payout to reward the extended effort. The entire concept is to reward strong performance and keep everyone focused on results, but keep enough profit to reinvest from a capital standpoint. This method also helps employees understand that companies do have to reinvest to remain competitive in the marketplace.

Other rules and stipulations for incentive programs must be clearly spelled out, such as what happens if an employee leaves the company, but has earned some incentive for the period. At the end of this chapter, you will find a sample document that spells out what happens under different scenarios.

How Does It Work?

The first step is to set up the program tables. In multiple-terminal companies, the first step in this process is to classify terminals by size. For example, a terminal manager who runs a 100-door terminal in Chicago that puts out 70 P&D drivers a day should certainly receive a higher payout than a manager who runs a 10-door terminal in Paducah, Kentucky that puts out 5 P&D drivers a day.

So, step one is to determine terminal classification. There are six classes of terminals, from Class 1 (smallest) to Class 6 (largest).

Table # 1:			
Terminal Classification Scale:			
Class 1	0 Units	To	3 Units
Class 2	4 Units	To	6 Units
Class 3	7 Units	To	11 Units
Class 4	12 Units	To	14 Units
Class 5	15 Units	To	20 Units
Class 6	21 Units	And	Over

Terminal class is determined based on two criteria: population and expected hours in pickup and delivery. Expected hours is a calculation from the TPG pickup and delivery system. That system measures the capacity and capacity utilization in P&D and generates a number called Management Performance, a measure of operating efficiency. The TPG program takes the net hours (time on the street of all drivers) and divides net hours by the Management Performance number to calculate the hours the terminal should have used at 100% efficiency. This method equalizes all terminals so one terminal that is grossly inefficient and uses more hours than needed does not have an advantage over another terminal that is efficient. It ensures we're comparing apples to apples.

Looking at the table below, a terminal that operates in an area that has a population between 50,001 and 100,000 people would get three units as the population factor (difficulty of operation). Population can be determined using Standard Metropolitan Statistical Area (SMSA) data published by the United States government.

Table # 2:				
Population Factors				
Determined By Location				
	0	To	25,000	1 Unit
	25,001	To	50,000	2 Units
	50,001	To	100,000	3 Units
	100,001	To	250,000	4 Units
	250,001	To	500,000	5 Units
	500,001	To	750,000	6 Units
	750,001	To	1,000,000	7 Units
	1,000,001	To	1,500,000	8 Units
	1,500,001	To	2,000.00	9 Units
	2,000,001	And	over	10 Units

The next chart used to determine the class of terminal is the Expected Hours calculation.

If the terminal has between 401 and 600 expected hours in P&D, the terminal would get four units for Expected Hours.

Table # 3:

Expected Hours Factors
Based On Weekly Expected Hours

0	To	100	1 Unit
101	To	200	2 Units
201	To	400	3 Units
401	To	600	4 Units
601	To	800	5 Units
801	To	1,000	6 Units
1,001	To	1,300	7 Units
1,301	To	1,700	8 Units
1,701	To	2,000	9 Units
2,001	To	2,500	10 Units
2,501	To	3,000	11 Units
3,001	To	3,500	12 Units
3,501	To	4,000	13 Units
4,001	To	4,500	14 Units
4,501	To	5,000	15 Units
5,001	And	over	16 Units

The next step, using the tables above, is to determine the class (size) of the terminal.

In this example, the terminal has three units based on its geographic area of operation, and the terminal receives four units for weekly expected hours.

Works Hours
Classification
Expected Hours
Baseline:
Table # 4

Terminal	Net Hours	MGT Ratio	Exp Hrs	Workdays	Exp Hrs Per Day	Exp. Hrs Per Week	Exp Hrs Units	Pop Units	Total Units	Class
1	6515.21	120.57	5403.67	21	257.32	1287	7	10	17	5
2	1808.62	127.93	1413.76	21	67.32	337	3	4	7	3
3	1758.75	117.01	1503.08	21	71.58	358	3	4	7	3
4	1463.00	131.88	1109.34	21	52.83	264	3	4	7	3
5	1643.45	120.14	1367.95	21	65.14	326	3	4	7	3
6	1751.20	125.37	1396.83	21	66.52	333	3	4	7	4
Total	14940.23	134.25	11128.66	21	449.04	2245				

This terminal would fall in the 7-to-11-unit category, so the terminal is a Class 3 terminal.

Now that we have established the class (size) of the terminal, we must establish the job codes for participants and create a unit value for each position for each class of terminal. Every employee from the CEO down participates in the program; I have kept our example at the terminal level for illustration.

Table # 6: Job Point	Location Classification					
Job Code (See Table #6	Class 1	Class 2	Class 3	Class 4	Class 5	Class 6
1	1.5	2.5	3.5	4.0	5.0	6.0
2	N/A	N/A	1.75	1.75	3.00	4.00
3	N/A	N/A	1.75	1.75	2.50	3.00
4	1.00	1.00	1.25	1.25	1.50	2.00
5	1.25	1.25	1.25	1.25	1.25	1.25
6	0.75	0.75	1.00	1.25	1.25	1.50

As you can see from the example above, the size or class of the terminal determines the amount of points available, and each point is assigned a monetary value based on the total participants in the company (terminals, maintenance, corporate, clerical, and so on). For example, a terminal manager at a Class 3 terminal is eligible for 3.5 points. If the determined dollar value per point is $500.00, the manager would be eligible for a $1,750 bonus check. However, the payout can be reduced based on the level of performance in several areas.

In my view, a terminal manager is responsible for two primary objectives: to grow the revenue base of the terminal and to improve profitability. The manager's objectives would be different from an inbound supervisor's. The inbound supervisor might be held responsible for claims, on-time delivery performance, pickup and delivery productivity, and return shipments. Each one of the categories would equate to 25% of the available bonus. Also keep in mind that the categories can be changed from bonus timeframe to bonus timeframe, based on areas that need improvement.

Table # 6
Job Code Legend
1. **Terminal Manager**
2. **Assistant Terminal Manager / AM & PM Supervisor**
3. **Dispatchers**
4. **P&D Driver**
5. **Linehaul Driver**
6. **Dock Workers**

Management Performance	
	% Points Earned
115	100%
115.5	95%
116	90%
116.5	85%
117	50%
117.5	25%
117	20%
Over 117	0%

The table above represents pickup and delivery productivity. Management Performance, using the TPG P&D productivity measurement, measures the supervision of the terminal that plans, organizes, and controls the P&D operation. Driver performance is handled differently. The purpose of the Management Performance goal is to get supervisors and drivers working on improving performance together as a team. One of the criteria for the driver to receive their bonus is Management Performance.

In the table above, 115 is a level of inefficiency that represents a 15% inefficiency in the P&D operation. You might be asking yourself, "Why not 100, which is perfect?" The answer is, this is a journey! Goals should be achievable and incremental. In the example above for our Class 3 terminal, the supervisor has 1.75 points.

If each point value is worth $500.00, the supervisor is eligible for a bonus of $875.00 ($500.00 x 1.75 = $875). Of the $875.00, P&D Management Performance represents $218.75 of the supervisor's total bonus ($875 x 0.25 = $218.75). If the supervisor achieved a Management Performance of 117, he or she would be paid $109.38 for P&D performance ($218.75 x 0.50 = $109.38).

This is just an example of the criteria for an inbound supervisor. Again, each position or department within the company would have its own criteria. Account representatives might have 50% of the bonus payout tied to quality of revenue, 15% tied to a terminal revenue goal, and 35% tied to their territory revenue goal.

The purpose of a performance-based incentive program is to keep everyone on the same page and motivated to perform so the company can continue to grow, serve the customer, improve profitability, and reward the members of the company for their efforts in making that happen. As a coach, one of your biggest fears is having a player playing for his own stats, which is why unit and team goals are celebrated. The criteria should be meaningful and achievable, but pretty tight. Another thing you learn as a coach is that the behavior you reward is the behavior you get back. Don't reward mediocrity! Challenge your people to perform at meaningful levels. I guarantee you they will feel better about themselves!

Below you will find a sample program rules document to give you a feel for how this kind of program is administered. While the methodology is the same, the program is customizable from carrier to carrier.

PERFORMANCE-BASED COMPENSATION PLAN

The primary objective of a Performance-based Compensation Plan is to energize and align the leaders of the organization with the Vision of the organization.

A company must, during the process, balance value to the customer, the associates, and re-investment in the organization.

A. Participants in the Plan

All full-time, salaried LTL Division, Corporate, Maintenance, and Safety associates of Client T should be eligible for plan participation.

B. Plan Guidelines and Computations

1. **Point System:** Each position carries a point values that varies. The variation is based on the responsibility that the position has toward the performance outlined in the plan and the classification of the Service Center, defined by the location and productive work of the Service Center.

2. **Monthly Payout Amount:** The payout for "potential" distribution to participants in the plan is a share of the LTL Division profits, which is computed as follows:
    a. A percentage of all operating income below the following schedule of LTL Division operating ratio: 2011 – 93, 2012 – 92, 2013 – 91, 2014 – 90
    b. If the LTL Division operates above the respective increments outlined in item (a.) above, there will be no distribution.
    c. Operating expenses include any amount of payout from the previous period.
    d. Operating expenses exclude any extraordinary items that in the opinion of the President /CEO and CFO distort the earnings computed.
    e. It is anticipated that earnings computed for this plan be the same as computed under existing GAAP (Generally Accepted Accounting Principles).

3. **Point Value:** Each month, a point value will be computed by dividing the monthly payout (see number 2, above) by the total number of points in the plan (see number 1, above). The total point values will be used to compute the amount of payout earned by individual participants.

4. **Success Measurements:** Key monthly performance measurements that are critical to the operational and financial health of Client T will be assigned to groups of participants. The measurements assigned to each group will vary based on the job responsibilities of each group. Results will be computed and converted to a total percentage achievement, ranging from 0 to 100% for each individual participant in the plan. The measurements assigned to Service Center Managers, Service Center Sales, Service Center Operations, and corporate participants, along with the conversion factors, are identified in Plan Tables.

C. Payout Distribution Earned by Participants

Payout Amount Earned: The individual point values (see section B, above) are multiplied by the job measurement percentages (see section B, number 4, above) to arrive at the total performance-based payout earned by each participant.

1. **Monthly Payout at 85% of Monthly Amount Earned:** Once the LTL Division profits from the previous month are calculated, an amount equal to 85% of the Incentive Earnings will be available to the participants. All applicable federal and state taxes will be withheld from the gross dollars paid.
2. **15% Held Back until End of Year:** If the company achieves its operating ratio goal, the remaining 15% will be distributed. If the company falls short of the goal operating ratio, the 15% will be used to move the company to its operating ratio goal. If any funds remain after this move, they will be distributed to participants.

Supplementary Policies

D. Integrity of Plan

Any participant who willingly falsifies or manipulates any measurement connected to the plan will be disqualified from future participation in the plan and will risk termination of employment.

E. Qualifying for Participation and/or Termination of Participation

1. **Full-time Job Assignment to Qualifying Position:** Regular, full-time work assignment determines the level of participation in the plan. A temporary assignment to another job responsibility will not

change the level of participation in the plan.

2. **New Employees Assigned to a Qualifying Position:** A new employee must be in the qualifying position for an entire calendar month that funds are being computed and distributed for.

3. **Termination of Employment:** Employee participation in the plan ends on the date employment is terminated, without regard to amounts that may have been earned up to the date of termination.
   a.   Non-qualifying Position to a Qualifying Position: The employee must be in the qualifying position for the entire calendar month funds are being computed and distributed for.
   b.   Qualifying Position to a Qualifying Position: The employee will participate in the old position during the calendar month of transfer and will start participating in the new position during the first complete calendar month in the new position.
   c.   Qualifying Position to Non-qualifying Position: The employee will participate in the old position through the last full month of employment in the old position. Amounts held in reserve will be carried in the name of the employee until the end of the fiscal year and distribution or forfeiture of the reserved amounts will be computed as prescribed for all participants in the plan.

F.   Confidentiality

All facets of this plan are to be kept strictly confidentiality. Any questions about the plan should be addressed in private to the participant's direct supervisor. Casual discussions about the plan or its contents are not to be carried on at any time. All matters associated with the incentive payout and payroll are private communications between the employee and their immediate supervisor. It is the intention of the company that this plan be handled with the same level of sensitivity. Failure to comply with this confidentiality clause may result in disqualification from the plan.

G.   Communication of Changes in Plan Assignment

All changes in job plan assignment will be communicated to payroll personnel through existing company policies, procedures, and forms. The information required by the form should contain all necessary information needed for plan participation. The effective date on the change of status becomes the official date for purposes of determining plan participation.

Job assignment changes, new hires, termination, transfers, and all other status changes that impact plan participation are to be communicated on the proper form, which becomes the official notice of record. All of the current procedures for processing the employee profile and profile update forms continue without any exceptions for purposes of participation in the plan.

H. Revisions to Plan and Assignment of Plan Document

1. **Date and Duration of Plan:** The plan becomes effective on September 1, 2011 and will continue in effect until it is terminated by the actions of the President/CEO. The plan year will be the fiscal year of the company.

2. **Intent and Right to Modify:** It is the intent of the President that the plan achieves the objectives outlined in the plan and continues from year to year. It is reasonable to expect changes and enhancements to this program. Additionally, the right to alter, reduce, expand, or terminate the plan at any time is reserved.

3. **Plan Document:** This document and contents of this document, including attachments, are to be kept strictly confidential and are not to be photocopied or distributed in any manner. This document is to be surrendered by the holder (Service Center Manager, Department Manager) to their supervisor upon termination of the holder's participation in the plan. If plan revisions are made, the entire document will be returned to the Plan Administrator.

PERFORMANCE-BASED COMPENSATION PLAN

I hereby acknowledge that I am in receipt of and have had the opportunity to read the Client T Performance-based Compensation Plan and that any questions regarding my understanding have been fully explained to me by my direct supervisor. I also understand my personal responsibility in maintaining the confidentiality clause of the Plan. The plan documents will remain the property of Client T Corporation.

Acknowledgement   Witness

_____   _____

Name   Date   Name   Date

PERFORMANCE-BASED COMPENSATION PLAN

Performance Measurements

1. **Service Center Manager: Job Code 1**
   a. Service Center Operating Ratio   50%
   b. Service Center Revenue Achievement   50%

2. **Assistant Service Center Manager: Job Code 2**
   a. Service Center MGMT Performance   50%
   b. Service Center Loss & Damage Ratio   25%
   c. Service Center On-time I/B Service   25%

3. **Service Center Account Manager: Job Code 3**
   a. Service Center Operating Ratio   50%
   b. Service Center Revenue Achievement   15%
   c. Account Manager Revenue Achievement   35%

4. **Operations Manager: Job Code 4**
   a. Service Center MGMT Performance   50%
   b. Service Center Loss & Damage Ratio   25%
   c. Service Center On-time I/B Service   25%

5. Front Line Supervisor/Dispatcher: Job Code 5
   a. Service Center Missed Pickups   50%
   b. Service Center Loss & Damage Ratio   25%
   c. Service Center On-time I/B Service   25%

6. President/CEO
   a. Company Operating Ratio   50%
   b. ROI   50%

7. Region Manager
   a. Company Operating Ratio   50%
   b. Company Revenue Achievement   30%
   c. ROI   20%

8. Quality/Human Resources Department
   a. Company Operating Ratio   50%
   b. ROI   50%

9. Accounting Department
   a. Company Operating Ratio   50%
   b. ROI   50%

10. MIS Department
   a. Company Operating Ratio   50%
   b. ROI   50%

11. Corporate Account Manager
   a. Company Operating Ratio   50%
   b. Company Revenue Achievement   50%

12. Safety Department
   a. FMCSA Rating   50%
   b. Hours of Service   50%

13. Claims Department
   a. Company Operating Ratio   50%
   b. Claims Ratio   50%

14. Traffic/Pricing Department
   a. Company Operating Ratio   50%
   b. Company Revenue Achievement   50%

15. **Director of Maintenance, Maintenance Dept.**
    a.   FMCSA Rating   50%
    b.   Company On-time I/B Service   50%

16. **Supervisor, Maintenance Department**
    a.   FMCSA Rating   50%
    b.   Roadside Equipment Failure   30%
    c.   Company On-time I/B Service   20%

17. **Manager of Linehaul, Linehaul Department**
    a.   Company Operating Ratio   40%
    b.   Company On Time Departures   30%
    c.   Company On-time Arrivals   30%

18. **Supervisor, Linehaul Department**
    a.   Company On-time Departures   40%
    b.   Company On-time Arrivals   40%
    c.   Equivalent Empty Trailers   20%

CHAPTER 8

DEVELOPING AND IMPLEMENTING
A COHERENT STRATEGY

Without a strategy the organization is like a ship without a rudder, going around in circles. It's like a tramp, it has no place to go. And incidentally, such platitudes as "make a profit" or "increase market share" do not provide the unified direction we are seeking.

—Joel E. Ross and Michael J. Kami

You Must Be a Sales and Marketing Organization

Ted Turner once said, "Early to bed, early to rise, work like hell and advertise." Growth is the panacea of business; companies either grow or decay. Do not adopt a strategy of growth for growth's sake. You must have the systems and people in place and be smart about how you grow!

I do *strongly* suggest to all my clients that they adopt a philosophy of being a sales and marketing organization that just happens to make money handling freight. If you have a structure in place that drives growth in your company, many potential problems are solved. Growth sets the company up to be in a position to do really exciting things because it has more resources available. On the other hand, if it's shrinking, the company will not be able to accomplish all its goals because it will lack an abundance of resources. The President or CEO's job is to create an atmosphere in which growth is seen as the lifeblood of the business.

Growth, either organic or through acquisitions, should be the basic mindset, and that mindset must permeate the entire organization, since it is essential for the company to remain a viable competitor. As the President or CEO, you must have that at the forefront of all your thinking. As a leader it is important to know that if you have a slow-growth or stagnant company, you will not get the blue-chip people, the atmosphere will not be exciting, and you'll always be cutting, cutting, cutting—and that is not a fun environment to be a part of. I strongly suggest you make growth a way of life for your company.

Once you make that decision, as the Nike commercial says, just do it! It's all about execution. As a coach you learn quickly that you can have to best game plan in all of football, but if your team cannot execute the game plan, it's going to be a long afternoon. Bottom line: It's all about how well you and your company execute the growth plan, how effectively you get it done.

Do you have a costing and operations system within the company that ties execution to the growth strategy? Do you have a blueprint to work from to build the company? You must have a system in place that loops back and around, so that every time you do something you can see how it contributes to the strategy, and so that you can ensure that every decision you make meets a strategic objective. Also, what is the timeline for the milestone you're moving toward—the achievement of the objective?

I see in many companies that strategy is divorced from execution. Every goal, every milestone must be tied to your strategic objective and you must be able to measure team members' performance. When you measure, you get results. Communication is key and you must make certain that what you want is clearly understood by every person in the company. It is also absolutely imperative that your strategy is tied to your compensation plan. If you're going to be successful, you really have to yell and exaggerate the importance of your strategy, as well as reward the people in the organization who work hard to help the company grow.

A Real-life Example

A new client company that had implemented the system became stagnant, and profitability was declining. The senior management team was pretty sound and they knew they needed to take a look at what they were doing and re-evaluate their strategy. The company had grown to a pretty large organization through partnering with other carriers, a strategy that had served them well for a couple of decades.

In going through the numbers, the first area that jumped out at me was their low revenue per shipment and low contribution dollars per shipment. Since the majority of their business was partner and interline, revenue per shipment was split between the carriers involved. Some of the splits were based on D83 and some were simple 50/50 revenue splits, hence the lower revenue per shipment. The shipment growth percentage was outpacing the revenue percentage of growth by a substantial amount.

The company has multiple terminals in several states, so we used the costing system to segment the customer base and found that the partner business was outgrowing their direct terminal-to-terminal business. Once we analyzed the direct business, we found that the revenue per shipment and contribution dollars per shipment were very strong, almost twice as much in many cases. The conclusion was that the more the client's partner business grew, the worse the client's margins would become.

Also, the operations department was struggling to control cost. They had the TPG productivity system in place, which told us they had plenty of capacity in P&D, yet they kept throwing more trucks and more people at the problem. It turned out that the operations executive did not believe in the system and continued to use his own outdated methods, paradigms, seat-of-the-pants plans, and more spreadsheets than Microsoft could provide to create measurements. Operations was measuring everything and nothing was important. They stayed totally confused, and as a result, variable cost continued to rise.

The CEO and owner of this company is a future-based executive, and a great leader! He knew what he wanted to accomplish and is not afraid to deal with obstacles. As a result, he brought in a new VP of Operations. The new operations executive is sharp and focused. To make a long story short, he turned the operations department around. Pickup and delivery and dock efficiencies began improving and we saw variable cost as a percent of revenue begin dropping. One obstacle down.

As I noted, the management team is pretty sharp and knew the company was stagnant and needed to get some growth going. They had contacted one of their partners about acquiring them, and the other company was interested. I was concerned about this idea because both companies were not doing well financially, and I knew merging two companies is tough to do on many levels in the best of circumstances. Been there, done that, as they say! The primary reason, based on my experience, is that it takes a long time for two cultures to blend together. When both companies are struggling financially, cash and time are likely to run out. Another major reason for the failure of an acquisition or merger is a tendency to overestimate sales and underestimate costs.

However, we decided to take a look. After all the confidentiality agreements and other paperwork items were signed, we were able to dive into the other company. One of my major concerns was the quality of their customer base. We also wanted to note the trend in their variable cost as a percent of revenue and the trends of revenue per shipment, variable cost per shipment, and contribution dollars per shipment. As expected, the revenue per shipment, variable cost per shipment, and contribution dollars per shipment were trending in the wrong direction.

We had income statements, driver manifests, and other data, so we calculated wage and fringe cost per hour and other unit costs and were able to set those up in the cost model to look at the customer base. After building in a reasonable margin of error, we concluded the other company's customer base was a huge part of their problem. They too had the same strategy of growing through partnerships, and the numbers just did not work any longer.

After looking at the numbers, the financial position of both companies, the fundamentals, and culture, it was decided it was just too risky for both companies. You must always remember: Fundamentals are enduring!

So we went back to the drawing board. After many conversations, iterations of numbers, soul searching, and good old common sense, it was decided that the safest and best course of action would be to focus on growing the direct business through the sales team.

As that strategy unfolded, the numbers began improving. The costing/pricing executive understood the key relationships and made good decisions about new business. It wasn't all profitable, but he clearly understood cost, volume, and contribution well enough that he made great decisions with regard to the opportunities the sales team brought to the table.

Back to operations. The new VP and his team used the system, believed the excess capacity the system demonstrated we had was correct, and were able to absorb most of the new growth with capacity already in place.

Meanwhile, the owner put in place an incentive compensation program and has had a ball rewarding his team. The program includes everyone in the organization.

As a result of their efforts, and the courage and focus of the team, two years later the company is extremely profitable and has navigated a tremendous turnaround. They're going to be fine! In fact, perhaps they should revisit their original strategy of acquiring another company. They have put together what I call a future-based company.

That was an overview from 40,000 feet. To get into every detail would take another book, and I'm done after this one!

We could create that strategy and execute because we knew the company's costs, capacity, and capacity utilization, so we understood the company's strengths and weaknesses, which allowed us to put our strategy on paper and develop it in a coherent fashion.

Don't you just love it when a plan comes together?

Before You Can Develop a Philosophy or Strategy, You Must Understand Your Costs

While some of this chapter re-visits parts of earlier chapters, I feel it imperative that you, the reader, without any doubt whatsoever, understand the importance of truly knowing your costs, capacity and capacity utilization in order to develop a strategy and philosophy of who you really are as a company. If you do not understand your costs, you cannot execute on any strategy you create. You're guessing! You must understand not only the cost numbers that are on an income statement, but also the true unit costs that drive the numbers on the income statement, and how to manage them for profitability.

I have found many companies that are excellent at defining their tactical or operational goals and direction, but fail to have them tied to a definitive overarching growth strategy. I have also found many companies that are excellent at defining and communicating their strategy, but fall far short of having that strategy aligned with tactical or operational goals.

I often find that a company's current cost model is a big factor in limiting its ability to truly understand its costs. As a prelude to understanding strategy, we will revisit the shortcomings of traditional cost models and why they prevent the carrier from creating a coherent strategy that aligns with tactics, which is essential in building a competitive advantage.

The missing piece of current cost models is the ability to measure and define capacity and capacity utilization. An LTL carrier is a very capital-intense organization, and that intensity is driven by the capacity we invest to provide service to our customers. Once more, capacity is defined as P&D, dock/platform, and line-haul, as well as all the ancillary costs incurred to provide that capacity to the marketplace. I find that 66 to 72 cents of every revenue dollar is consumed by those three cost centers.

Financial statements assume the carrier is operating at 100% capacity. Activity-based costing (ABC) and fully allocated costing systems also assume the carrier is operating at 100% capacity and therefore assign too much cost to customers and shipments. Since traditional cost models cannot measure capacity or utilization, they seriously hamper the planning process.

Traditional cost-based models calculate cost driver rates assuming the company is operating at full capacity. However, operations at full capacity are extremely rare. Cost driver rates should be calculated at practical capacity, not actual utilization. **The major flaw with those costing systems is they cannot measure the potential value of unused capacity in the costing/pricing process.**

Thus they over-cost shipments, taking valuable, much-needed market share off the plate. If your costing system cannot measure capacity and capacity utilization you also overspend on new equipment purchases.

Using capacity-based costing (CBC), the carrier knows exactly how much additional business can be absorbed with current capacities. If a terminal has a P&D management performance of 135, this tells leadership the terminal can handle 35% more work with the capacity and cost already in place (drivers, tractors, trailers, etc.). Imagine the impact on profitability that would have.

Several leaders have told me that their in-house or ABC system was not accurate or granular enough to capture the operational complexity of an LTL carrier.

Every carrier I have worked with over the last 28 years has had a minimum of 30% excess capacity in P&D, 12 to 15% in dock operations, and if the carrier is a short- to medium-haul region carrier, at least 35 to 40% excess capacity in linehaul. Not being able to quantify capacity and capacity utilization severely hampers the ability of the carrier to align strategy and tactics. Not being able to quantify that gap puts carriers in the position of overspending on capital investments and also prevents the carrier from understanding the growth that can be absorbed without adding additional capacity, which is the key to building long-term sustainable profitability.

Measuring Fundamentals That Drive Costs Is Critical

For a costing system to be useful in developing a strategy, it must feature time consumption in pickup and delivery and dock operations (those employees are paid by the hour, and miles driven in pickup and delivery consume time) and weight, cube, distance, and lane balance in linehaul to measure capacity and capacity utilization as central components. As stated above, those three areas consume 66 to 72% of every revenue dollar. A capacity-based costing method identifies the size of profit opportunities available for capture. Not to sound like an advertisement, but the TPG capacity-based costing model is the only cost model in the industry that measures the carrier's total capacity and capacity utilization.

In pickup and delivery, time is a common measurement, based on the miles driven, geographical area, and mix of work performed on the trip. On the dock, time is determined by the physical size of the dock and the mix of freight moving through. Also, inbound time to handle a particular shipment is different from outbound, or sort and seg, appointment, and so on. Unlike other systems, which focus on the customer as the unit of analysis, a costing system must work directly at the transaction level to measure time consumption. Time equations measure how different shipments consume time and capacity, and time algorithms are able to measure transaction complexity. This method provides the carrier with an accurate model of the cost and profitability of producing and delivering their service and managing customer relationships.

In order to develop a strategy that will build competitive advantage, a costing system must provide different levers for measuring and implementing a strategy. If a company's scorecard describes a low-cost, efficient (not low-price) strategy need, a costing system must have the capability to measure capacity and capacity utilization to measure the critical processes that drive growth and profitability. Otherwise the company runs the risk of implementing a low-cost strategy with incomplete and faulty information about their fundamental cost elements.

The Customer Base—Again

Capacity-based costing allows the company the ability to measure profitability simply and accurately at the individual shipment and customer level, enabling the carrier to consider new metrics such as the percentage of customers that do not cover out-of-pocket costs, the percentage of customers that provide contribution to fixed costs and overhead but are not profitable, and the percentage of customers that are profitable. This capability allows carriers to measure the magnitude of losses of unprofitable customer relationships and to focus the planning strategy on managing customers and customer-base growth for profits, not just for sales.

Capacity-based costing gives companies a practical option for accurately determining the cost and capacity utilization of operations and the profitability of their customers. This allows managers to set priorities for cost improvements and processes, rationalize their customer base mix, price customers' business, and manage customer relationships.

The recession has left fewer, but considerably stronger major LTL carriers in the marketplace, putting smaller local and regional carriers at the mercy of their pricing. **It has never been more important in our history for local and regional carriers to know their true operating costs.**

A costing system that measures capacity and capacity utilization provides leaders with the capability of forecasting the future. The time equations capture the major factors that create demand for capacity, including changes in operating efficiencies, customer volume and mix, and lane and geographic profitability.

Capacity-based costing using time algorithms allows leaders to perform dynamic what-if analyses for various scenarios. The model is easily incorporated into the budgeting process, calculating the required capacity and spending needed to provide capacity to deliver on future periods' sales and operations plans, and also enables leaders to determine the level of staffing needed to deliver the service requirements. The model allows the company to get away from the useless, antiquated class-rate system and develop its own tariff based on its own cost.

The first step in developing a long-term strategy is to know the cost of providing your service to the marketplace. If you do not have a costing model that measures capacity and capacity utilization, you limit your ability to truly understand your cost and the company's strengths and weaknesses.

In order to develop a coherent strategy that builds competitive advantage, you must know how to *position* your organization in the markets it operates in. Next you have to know the *capabilities* you can leverage. Once you understand those, you can now develop a strategy and plan that *neutralizes* your competition.

If your costing model cannot measure operational capacity and capacity utilization, the likelihood is that you will implement a strategy that is flawed and not aligned with tactics. Probably frustration will ensue, and the strategy will be put on the shelf and forgotten. It's back to business as usual ... until the third quarter of next year. If you're going to develop a strong strategic direction and a budget to complement your strategy, know your cost, and know your capacity and capacity utilization!

Developing a Strategy Is Not Magic or Voodoo

Strategy is not some mysterious, esoteric, complex, daunting word requiring a guru or mystic to define. It's really pretty basic! In fact, it is simply deciding how you want to compete and then making clear-cut choices about how to accomplish that.

Once you complete this strategizing, you can then think about what is standing in your way. In an earlier chapter I wrote about a phenomenon called the "Barrier of Complexity." What are the top barriers that are creating the complexity in your organization, keeping you from defining and achieving your strategy?

Most companies think that creating a strategy or plan will complete the process, putting brackets around the future. They place the plan on the shelf, feeling blissful and secure knowing they have defined what they want to be or do. They think it will "automagically" occur! Guess what? Actually, a very high percentage of companies fail to achieve their strategy and goals. The main reason is that defining a strategy is not the end. Strategy is not static; it is a living, breathing, ever-changing game that is fun and alive!

Defining a strategy is defining how you're going to win, and that requires focus and continuous planning because the operating environment is always changing, becoming more complex and moving to a higher level. Your strategy must keep evolving to face your company's challenges.

When I was coaching college football, I was promoted from coaching nose tackles to defensive line coach. I remember the head coach calling me in and having a talk with me about my new responsibilities. During that conversation he told me something that is so true that I have lived by it my entire adult life.

The conversation went something like this: He asked how I liked coaching football. My reply was, "I love it; getting to do this is absolutely amazing!" He then put life (and football and business) in perspective. He said, "Coach, you have the responsibility for the defensive line now, and that is a huge responsibility. As the line of scrimmage goes, so goes the game! Games are won and lost on the line of scrimmage." His next comments changed my life. "Coach Sullivan, the game is always changing and moving to a higher level. You now have to make the personal commitment to continue to learn and grow so you can continue to achieve. If you don't do that, the game will pass you by and your value to this team will begin to diminish."

Wow! Pretty powerful, isn't it? I have found that is so true in the business world. Coach was right!

Implementing your organization's strategy requires the very same kind of leadership; achieving your strategy requires your focus to be sharp. Although your strategy may be clear, how you get there requires adjustments. Not to inundate you with football analogies, but there is a halftime in football. After half the game time has elapsed, the coaches for both teams make adjustments to their original game plan for the second half based on how the game unfolded in the first half.

It is no different in business relative to achieving your strategy. A football game has four quarters and a business has four quarters. You not only have to make adjustments, but you also have to take action and execute! Planning with no action creates frustration and failure. Coaches make sure their players understand the game plan and adjustments so they can bring it to life and execute it.

The same holds true for business leaders. As a coach, you learn very quickly that no matter how badly the game is going on a Saturday afternoon, you can't step onto the field and play the game for your players. Good coaches prepare and teach their strategy and philosophy to the players and then coach like hell so they are able to execute. The leader of a business must do the same with their department heads and employees.

A well-defined and clear strategy and philosophy set the foundation for success. I know a coach who won a national championship in then-Division I (now FBS) college football. His philosophy was this: His defense would be extremely physical and aggressive and would set up his offense with good field position by focusing on three and out (denying the opponent third-down success), creating turnovers, and not giving up big plays. His special teams were disciplined and his offense just would not make mistakes! His team was undefeated and won a national championship with that clear-cut, simple strategy. He built his coaching staff around that strategy and recruited players who would fit his system.

That is an example of how a simple, clear strategy sets the foundation for success and clearly communicates how you're going to play the game and differentiate your organization from the competition. A clear-cut strategy creates a laser-like focus that aligns all levels of the organization, which keeps every department focused and energized.

A clear strategy allows a carrier to measure and evaluate its strengths (and weaknesses) against what is happening outside the organization in the marketplace. Basically, it reduces complexity down to the unique elements needed to excel. Having a breathing, living strategy positions the company to be able to move quickly and decisively to keep up with changing conditions.

Research has shown that no company is able to effectively work on more than three or four key focus areas at the same time. The more you dilute your effort, the slower the progress you will make. You cannot be everything to everybody, regardless of how much money you have.

I give companies these three instructions for creating an effective strategy:

1. Come up with a huge "That's it," or a new direction for the company.

2. It's all about people! That's all you've got. Get the right people in the right position to drive your new direction forward.

3. Passionately and with unbridled determination, build a philosophy that as leaders, employees and a company, we must be better today than we were yesterday.

Strategy is determining how you're going to differentiate yourself from the competition. Also, your strategy must be difficult to replicate.

Answer the following questions.

1. What is your current and future competitive advantage?

2. Do you have a system in your company that aligns all departments to your strategy?

3. How do you know?

Finally, strategy is all about finding that great idea. Once you have that, you put a passionate team behind it, and push that team to search every day. Accomplishing that will create a winning strategy without volumes of books and lots and lots of convoluted discussions.

What about your people? Are you winning the blue chippers? Are your people holding you back? Are your people continuing to develop themselves? Who's getting the best people, and are they staying? Are your people staying? How is your bench strength versus that of your competition? How do your people stack up against your competition?

Now, be your competitor. How would your competitors see you? How would they describe your talent? Are you constantly evaluating your team? Do a deep dive back into your organization and be honest about it. Continuous evaluation is one of the greatest things of all time. Give your own organization an honest look! What are you missing, not seeing? What are you missing and not seeing in understanding your competitors and their actions?

Do you have a clear vision of the playing field now? Does everyone in the organization see the same things you see? Do you understand the things that do not make sense? Do you understand and have you checked the important facts and assumptions? Be certain not to overcomplicate. Once you're certain you have a clear picture, get moving!

Remember, strategy is nothing more than figuring out how you're going to compete. Once you determine that, execute!

CHAPTER 9

TURNING STRATEGY INTO ACTION

Set goals - high goals for you and your organization. When your orga-nization has a goal to shoot for, you create teamwork, people working for a common good.

—Coach Bear Bryant
University of Alabama

The Game Plan

As we discussed in the previous chapter, strategy is a breathing, living process that changes as the company moves through its life cycle. Companies evolve or they decline; that is inevitable in the world of business. Companies must understand this or they run the risk of being left behind. As a leader, going through the process of developing and implementing a strategy delivers the opportunity to understand the company much better.

You see, as companies grow, they go through evolutionary stages; within each stage of evolution revolutions occur in the form of obstacles or barriers. If companies' leaders do not have a strong belief in their strategies or are not disciplined enough to try to understand that these revolutions or barriers are normal and work through them, their confidence in their strategy weakens, and the "flavor-of-the-month" approach takes over: constant change, trying to find that magic bullet that will make the company profitable. At this point what I call management by thrashabout ensues, and soon it's back to business as usual. These companies become mired in mediocrity. They will do well in good economic times, but become highly vulnerable in bad economic times.

Implementing a strategy is not a sprint; it is a marathon. A person does not wake up one morning and say, "I'm going to run an 8-minute mile today" when that person has never even walked a 20-minute mile before. You have to go through stages, or evolve, to the point of being able to run an 8-minute mile through training and understanding the body and its limits. The same holds true for a company.

I have often worked with companies that were stagnant or declining from a profitability standpoint, with neutral or negative cash flow, and found that management decided the answer to their problems was "more revenue." That is the death rattle! Bringing in more revenue is a growth strategy and when a company is in the stagnant or declining stage, there is a reason for that; a growth strategy is not appropriate during this period. In the stagnant or declining stage, the company does not have the human, physical, and financial resources strong enough to support that growth strategy, and decline will accelerate.

In the last chapter I included three "concealed" elements that companies with effective strategies have in common. The second of these elements was the right people. I have no doubt, after 27 years of working with successful companies and stagnant and declining companies, that the quality of a company's people determines the level of financial resources available to a company, which in turn determines the magnitude and quality of its physical resources.

Strategy, Goals, and Execution

What we have done at TPG is develop a system that a carrier can use to implement their strategy and achieve their goals. This book, as the title suggests, provides the blueprint. Using the data generated from the TPG Capacity Based Costing Model, the carrier can align strategy with tactics, which dramatically increases the success percentage. What we try to do is look at a year as a season. As you know, football teams have a 12-game schedule. We have 12 months in a year. So we look at each month as a game and each week as a quarter. Using the data from the TPG System, we create a game plan, and just as a football coaching staff studies and grades the film after each game, we do the same with the company each month.

Understanding the game and leverage points is a must! As you know, all championship teams have a strong defense. The defense has several goals (like the offense) for the season and for each game as it arrives. However, there is one statistic that coaches know is really the measure of success defensively: *scoring defense*. If the opponent cannot score, they cannot beat you!

Coaches know that if you have to win games by outscoring your opponent (or growing revenue just for the sake of growing revenue, in a company), you should keep your résumé current because you aren't going to be around long. As we say in the South, that dog ain't gonna hunt! Most often a new coach who inherits a team works on the defense first. The defense develops faster than the offense, so having a strong defense buys time for the offense to develop. In fact there is a saying among coaches, and I am sure you've heard it before: Offense sells tickets and gets the crowd excited, and the defense wins big games and championships. It's a cliché, but it's true.

Scoring Defense for the LTL Carrier

Now for an LTL carrier, the statistic for scoring defense is variable cost as a percent of revenue. That's the granddaddy of them all! As stated earlier, the goal is to continuously drive that number down. That is the key statistic that determines the level of profitability for an LTL carrier. I consider operations defense and sales and marketing as offense. We begin the journey to a championship status by improving the relationship of variable cost to revenue, generating a higher level of contribution dollars to cover fixed cost, semi-fixed cost, and overhead.

If we can manage that key relationship—percent of variable cost to revenue—the percentages are extremely high we'll win. If your operations department can manage their cost and capacity on a daily basis, you will have a strong chance of dominating your opponents. So, P&D, dock/platform, and linehaul are the key activities in variable cost that you have to control. It's all about capacity and capacity utilization. Those three activities make up 97% of that all-important ratio: percent of variable cost to revenue.

Pulling It All Together

What I am going to do in the remainder of this chapter is make you think. Below I am illustrating a process many teams use. I am going to take a season that the coaching staff, sat down and put together to give you an idea of the process. I purposely did not use "business" goals in this example because I want you to think and come up with your own goals. I did not want to provide examples for you. I want you to make a template from this as an exercise. I will also include how you actually break down a game. I want you to create your own method using this as a template. Make a template to use in your company or terminal each month. A great man named W. Clement Stone used an acronym that I use and suggest you use as you go through this process: R2A2. That stands for recognize, relate, assimilate, and apply.

As you work through the remainder of this chapter, think about your own company, terminal, or department and use the R2A2 formula to see if you can think of a strategy or goals that you can apply to your company or terminal.

VISION: Continue to learn and grow as teachers and coaching staff to prepare our players for success in life after football and college.

STRATEGY:

1. MODEL SOUND CHARACTER
Loyalty
Work ethic
Professionalism
Integrity
Respect for staff and players

2. PROMOTE
Vision of what is possible
Belief in total program
Positive behavior and attitude
Confidence
Team unity
Accountability to self and team

3. DEVELOP
Each player's ability to the fullest
Professional growth as a coaching staff

TEAM GOALS:
1. Conference championship
2. No off-field incidents
3. Unity
4. Play one game at a time
5. Play one play at a time
6. Be the most mentally and physically prepared team in the conference
7. Team grade point average of 2.9 and higher
8. Undefeated season

OFFENSIVE STRATEGY/PHILOSOPHY
1. Multiple sets and motion
   a. Option football
   b. Power football
2. Physical football
   a. Everyone blocks
   b. All ball carriers run through
3. Emphasize execution
   a. Low turnover ratio

  b. Minimal mistakes

  c. High repetition in practice

4. Efficient passing game

  a. 55% + completion

  b. 4% < interception

  c. One or fewer sacks per game

  d. Emphasis on play-action passing

5. Control football

OFENSIVE GOALS

1. Six or more yards per attempt
2. Pass completion of 55% or more
3. Average per pass seven yards or more
4. 38 points per game
5. Interception ratio 4% or less
6. One or zero turnovers per game
7. Third- and fourth-down conversion 45% or more
8. Penalties 20 yards or less per game
9. Knockdowns 1.5 per play
10. Score in the red zone 90% or more

DEFENSIVE STRATEGY/PHILOSOPHY

1. Aggressive, attacking defense
2. Play only one play at a time
3. Never take a play off
4. Force turnovers
5. Be a great tackling team
6. Score on defense

DEFENSIVE GOALS

1. Three yards per rushing attempt or fewer
2. Total yards 285 or less
3. Hold under 13 points per game
4. One or zero big plays (25 yards or more)
5. One sack for every eight passing plays
6. Stop 70% of third-down plays
7. Prevent touchdowns 70% inside red zone
8. Gain possession three or more times inside the 50-yard line

KICKING GAME

The kicking game will win the close ones.

1. Net punting 40 yards or more per game
2. Average punt return 10 yards or more per game
3. Kickoff coverage 23-yard line or less
4. Kickoff return average 28-yard line or more
5. Successful in 85% of all field goal attempts
6. Successfully kick all extra point attempts
7. No blocked punts on offense
8. Six or more blocked punts per season

The program strategy outlined above is the guiding light. Every week coaches not only grade the game played on Saturday, but also grade themselves as a coaching staff to see if the team is trending towards or away from the team strategy and program goals. Coaches will then determine which areas need more focus to achieve those goals.

Every carrier should have an overall strategy with program goals. Recall that strategy is not static; it is a breathing, living process that requires adjustments from time to time. That is why a carrier must not just develop a strategy and put it on the shelf. It should be a part of every weekly and monthly staff meeting.

As you know, teams play 12 games in a regular season, and so for each game a game plan is prepared for the opponent. The game plan outlines how the team is going to play their opponent and goals are set for each game that, if achieved, will take the team to a win. As a coach, you never say, "That will **probably** take us to a win." You develop a plan *knowing* you are going to win. Good coaches create a belief in every player on the team to expect to win every game without any doubt! That is the job of the senior staff in any organization, and it begins with the president/CEO.

Below I provide an example of an actual game played so you can see how the process works. Unfortunately, the team got clobbered in this game. I chose this particular game because it is a good example of having a sound strategy and game plan, but the team just couldn't execute on the field. Furthermore, as coaches, adjustments were not made during the game. As coaches say, "We got our noses bloodied." As bad as this game was, though, the team and coaching staff believed in the game plan, in each other as coaches, and in the players. You learn as a coach to put a bad game behind you and move forward.

The game plan was a good game plan, but it was just one of those Saturdays that make coaches gray prematurely. As a coach you learn very quickly that teams have bad games and players have bad plays. However you have to be honest with your assessment and analysis, learn from the mistakes and understand the good things accomplished. You then communicate and break the film down for each unit, each player, coaches and then let it go. That game is history. You have another game to prepare so you coach and teach on the field at practice.

And companies have bad months. However, you must not let that deter you or weaken your resolve or belief in your team and strategy. You review it, learn from it, and *let it go* because you have another game on Saturday at 1 p.m. and you better have your team prepared.

Names in the example below were excluded to protect the innocent!

How to read the worksheet:

The first statistic is the goal, and the second statistic reflects the attainment. For example, In "Red zone 60% Touchdowns: 100%," 60% is the goal and 100% is the attainment.

Post–Game Worksheet – Opponent B

Offensive Goals Made:
Red zone 60% touchdowns: 100%
Red zone scoring 80%: 100%

Offensive Goals Missed:
More than 150 yards rushing: 80
More than 4 yards per carry: 2.9
Fewer than 2 turnovers: 2
Fewer than 3 sacks: 3
More than 27 points: 7
More than 225 yards passing: 86
More than 20 first downs: 8
Better than 60% pass completion percentage: 39%

Defensive Goals Made:
Fewer than 200 yards passing: 108
Fewer than 18 first downs: 15

Defensive Goals Missed:
Fewer than 125 yards rushing: 224
Fewer than 3.5 yards per carry: 3.9

More than 3 sacks per game: 1
Fewer than 13 points: 24
Less than 55% pass completion percentage: 60%
More than 2 turnovers: 1
Red zone 40% touchdowns: 75%
Red zone scoring 70%: 100%
Penalty yardage fewer than 50: 5

Overall Report Analysis – Grades and Comments

Offense – Rushing Game:
Interior running game – For the first time all season, we were completely shut down. They jammed the box and tackled extremely well. I thought they looked stronger and quicker than us. Player X and Player Y had no room to run. Player Z did a great job of gap control.

Perimeter running game – They were too fast for us and again tackled very well. They strung Player X out and he was looking for the sideline often.

Option game – Not applicable.

Draws – We had some success early with the draws, but they made adjustments and shut it down.

Short-yardage running game – This was *awful*! We had 10 three-and-outs Saturday and did not get in short yardage enough.

Yards after contact – Player V and Player W could not break the gang tackling. They put eight or nine in the box and they suffocated any running game after contact.

Offense – Passing Game:
Pass protection – The protection was okay, but not great. Player Q (quarterback) looked unsettled all day.

Underneath passing game – Player Q was awful here. His short swing passes were off of the mark. He never gave receivers a chance to make runs after the catch on short passes because the balls were thrown to the wrong shoulder or were off the mark.

Intermediate passing game – Terrible! There has never been a receiver to ever play the game who could have caught most of the intermediate passes Saturday.

Vertical passing game – Non-existent! We did not try to get the ball downfield. I am not sure the protection would have allowed it, but there were not any vertical balls thrown. On third and long, Player Q checked down to the underneath guy all afternoon.

Screens – They limited us in the screen game.

Yards after catch – Almost non-existent.

QB on-time throws– Lack of composure hurt the passing game and its timing.

Offense Overall:
First-down yardage – Pathetic! We had only 45 yards on 31 first-down plays. That is 1.4 yards per first down. Of the 23 first-down passes, 15 resulted in 2 yards or less.

Third-down conversion – We were only 4 of 16 on third downs. We lost first down, so in turn we lost third down.

Big plays – None.

Trick plays – None.

Defense – Running Game:
Interior running game – They pounded us inside and Player 1 (opponent's quarterback) had a huge night behind a dominating offensive line.

Perimeter running game – They did not have to run on the perimeter except a couple of times and when they did, we lost containment and gave up huge runs. This area was a *big* disappointment.

Option game – Not applicable.

Draws – They came at us with a power running game instead of a finesse draw game.

Short-yardage running game – They converted on their last three short-yardage situations on third down and were 1 for 2 on fourth down.

Yards after contact – This was the winner for Opponent B. We could not wrap up Player 2 and he made our defense pay big time.

Defense – Passing Game:
Pressure – We had some pressure on Player 1 (opponent's quarterback), but they did not have to pass the ball often enough for it to matter.

Underneath passing game – They only threw the ball 15 times, but were successful on the underneath routes.

Intermediate passing game – They also hit some outs to their wide receivers for gains of seven, eight, and nine yards.

Vertical passing game – The only times they went vertical resulted in a dropped touchdown and a big play to the tight end.

Screens – Not applicable.

Passes broken up – Player J had the only breakup of the game for us.

Open field tackling – Poor! Player 2 ran with a purpose and we had no answer.

Defense Overall:
Tackling – Perhaps the poorest effort all season. Player 3 is a good back, but our linebackers made him look better with a poor tackling technique.

First-down yardage – They got 4 or more yards on 11 of their 28 first-down plays.

Third-down conversion – They were 6 out of 18 on third downs, but they had short yardage on three of them.

Limiting big plays – They had big plays in the running game and the passing game. Player 2 broke tackles and had 6 runs of 11 yards or more.

Special Teams:
Kickoff returns – Average. We had 21.7 yards per return, but really made nothing happen here.

Kickoff coverage – Excellent. One touchback and one 14-yard run.

Punt return/block – They did a nice job of limiting our punt-return game.

Punt coverage, snap, protection, punt, coverage – Snaps were good with the exception of one. Protection was great. Punts were below average and coverage was good.

Field goals, extra points, snaps, hold, protection, kick – On the only attempt, everything looked well executed.

Overall Team:
Energy, enthusiasm, leadership – This was perhaps the biggest disappointment. We had a hangover from the previous game. I looked at our schedule and I knew this would be a big test for us. As coaches we know you, "Don't let one loss beat you twice," but we let one loss beat us twice. We were not ready to play in a hostile environment.

Coaching:
Emotionally prepared – *Poor!* We walked into a hornets' nest and had few answers. This was a big game but only Opponent B got the message.

Game plan – We came into the game with a good game plan on both sides of the ball. I agree with Coach Alpha trying to run the football. It had worked all year and Player X and Player Y are our best football players. Unfortunately, after the running game was shut down, we made no adjustments. Defensively we faced poor field position and could not get off the field. I think the game plan was sound, but players did not execute because of poor tackling.

Adjustments – Offensively we could not adjust to their defensive coordinator's brilliant game plan. We did not throw the ball on first down until it was too late. We continued to go three and out and no adjustments were made.

Personnel – Injuries are catching up to us.

Time outs/clock management – For the first time all season, clock management and timeouts were *awful!* We had to call a time out before the first play and used all first-half timeouts in the first eight minutes of the game. We looked confused and unprepared.

Brutal honesty: It hurts at the moment, but if you use it in a positive manner and learn from it, it will make you better!

Pretty interesting process, isn't it? You first have to know what you want to accomplish. Next, you have to totally believe, without one ounce of doubt or hesitation, that you can and will achieve it. As I noted above, we expected to win every game. Our coaches believed that and so did our players.

I completely believe, without any doubt or hesitation, that an LTL carrier cannot become a market leader if it is not a leader in "scoring defense," or controlling variable cost as a percent of revenue. This statistic really determines the level of profitability.

I also know, without any doubt or hesitation, that if the carrier does not understand its cost, it cannot control its cost! You can have all the sexy technology and gadgets in the industry, but if you don't know your cost, you'll never reach market-leader status. I heard Bob Stoops at a coaching convention say that a team can have the greatest game plan and all the schemes, looks, and tricks, but the team that blocks the best, tackles the best, and makes fewer mistakes on Saturday afternoon will probably win the game. Fundamentals: They are enduring!

I also know, without any doubt or hesitation, that if you cannot measure capacity and capacity utilization in your pickup and delivery, dock/platform, and line-haul trailer utilization operations areas, you really do not know your cost. The old metrics carriers use are too macro and too outdated. Look at the level of detail above in the game plan. A carrier must be capable of putting together a game plan each month and have a system that provides metrics at a level of detail that enables the management to better understand their team and develop the company. Then at the end of each month, the management team will have the tools to break down the month's data into those all-important, fundamental areas that create success.

I believe the first step in building a strong company is developing an operations team that can manage and control that all-important number: variable cost as a percent of revenue. A company can grow 30%, but if it does not have a system that allows the operations team to understand its capacity and capacity utilization, variable cost increases, profit potential is grossly diluted, and the company gives up profit dollars in the form of continuing or increasing costs driven by operating inefficiencies. Companies need to make certain as they grow their revenue base that operations absorbs the increase with current capacity in place, not giving precious profit dollars away by allowing variable cost to increase.

I repeat the advice I received many years ago: Make the personal commitment to continue to learn and grow so you can continue to achieve and so your value to the team and organization will not diminish. Also, always expect to win—always!

CHAPTER 10

THE BLUEPRINT: BRINGING IT ALL TOGETHER

The best way to predict your future is to create it.

—Peter Drucker

H ere we are at the final chapter, where we'll summarize key points and tie it all together. The blueprint, if followed, will establish the groundwork for growth because it lays a solid foundation built on LTL fundamentals, and fundamentals are enduring.

Prelude

You might be wondering why the last two chapters about strategy and building a game plan were not the first two chapters of this book. I believe that a company must know where it is in the business cycle and understand its cost, capacity, capacity utilization, and customer base before strategy and tactics can be planned. Leaders have to really know people, both managers and employees. You see, when a company installs my TPG system, the first step is calculating basic unit costs such as wages and fringes, variable cost per mile, and the variable fixed income statement. The first action is to get the company up and going on the pickup and delivery program so we can see capacity and capacity utilization, and gauge productivity levels in the company and its terminals.

You may remember that at the beginning of this book I noted that if you are a local or regional carrier, you're going to get your operating leverage from and make money in the pickup and delivery operation. By getting this module up and running quickly, you can get the training behind you, and set some easy goals for the terminals to achieve. Doing this gives leaders some idea of who is going to embrace change and who isn't.

The next step is the dock program, followed by linehaul trailer utilization. As a senior manager, having this information and process in place will help you know your leaders and employees better, which ultimately will allow the company to develop a strategy that has a much higher chance of working than it would if you did not know your company and employs on a deep level. This is why the last two chapters covered strategy and game planning.

Implementing a strategy requires an understanding of the company. If you do not understand your costs, how they behave, and how to manage them, a strategy or philosophy cannot be implemented to the fullest.

Before we get to the blueprint, I feel I would be derelict in my responsibility to readers if I didn't preface the content of this chapter by saying once more that the most important step for you, the reader, is to make the personal commitment to continue to study, learn, and grow as a leader so you can continue to be successful. Make the personal commitment to become a student of the game because the game is always changing and moving to a higher level. Don't get left behind.

THE FORMULA

1. Develop a variable/fixed managerial income statement.

2. Identify which stage of the business cycle the company is currently in:
   a. Trauma
   b. Stabilization
   c. Return to Growth

3. Implement the TPG cost model that has the capability to measure capacity and capacity utilization in pickup and delivery, dock, and linehaul trailer utilization.

4. Generate revenue growth using the TPG capacity-based costing model that factors in the value of unused capacity.

5. Absorb revenue growth with cost and capacity already in place.

6. Measure management and supervision at the terminal level in controlling cost and absorbing revenue growth with current capacity in pickup and delivery, dock, and linehaul trailer utilization.

7. Build a more productive customer base through TPG Customer Base Analysis programs by segmenting customers into contribution categories.

8. Get everyone in the company on the same page by implementing the TPG performance-based incentive compensation program.

The eight steps above are the formula a carrier needs to develop a blueprint for building long-term profitability into the company.

Step 1: Develop a variable/fixed managerial income statement.

You're probably saying, "Hold on Sullivan, the first chapter was about putting decline and failure in perspective, but step one of the process is to develop a variable/fixed income statement?"

Yes, putting the variable/fixed income statement together based on the process we defined in Chapter 2 will give you a basic understanding of how to place your company on the success continuum. Once you see the trend of your variable cost, contribution dollars, revenue per shipment, variable cost per shipment, and contribution dollars per shipment, you will be more knowledgeable than when you begin the evaluation.

Be sure to look at the breakeven point using the methodology outlined in the chapter as well. Understanding how a change in variable cost also changes the breakeven point of the company is critical. If all carriers understood and monitored this relationship, fewer carriers would fail. That is your early warning signal! That key relationship (variable cost as a percentage of revenue), breakeven revenue, and shipments are critical to understand! Remember to check if shipment growth (as a percentage) is growing at a higher rate of change than revenue. That too is a key set of numbers to know and understand.

In Chapter 1 we studied the stages a company finds itself in on the success continuum because recognizing your position helps you understand the level of human, financial and physical resources available. Not understanding that position puts you in danger of developing a strategy the company cannot support due to the quality and quantity of resources currently in place. If you are bleeding cash, you cannot adopt a growth strategy unless you have the financial resources to stabilize the company. Remember, as the company moves through the evolutionary business cycles, revolutions will occur within the cycle and those revolutions eat up cash! Banks, and even private equity or investment companies, will only lend to a certain point—and believe me they know what that point is and when reached will pull the trigger.

In Chapter 9, I explained how football coaches come up with a game plan. In the same way, sit down and honestly and brutally evaluate where your company is on the success spectrum! That is the starting point. If you have any doubt, get a qualified outside source to help you figure it out; many outside resources are available. Do not risk falling into "management by thrashabout"! The percentages are against you. If you don't know where you are, how can you map out where you need to go next?

When developing your variable/fixed income statement, your mission is to identify as closely as possible those costs that will change on a one-to-one level when picking up or delivering a shipment or working a shipment across a terminal's dock, and the variable cost of moving a shipment in linehaul between terminals. Endeavor to identify those costs so you can understand how a change in volume or output will impact the variable costs in your company, which in turn will determine the level of contribution dollars you have left to cover fixed costs, semi-fixed costs, and overhead.

For example, equipment depreciation is not a variable cost. It can be considered a direct cost or fixed cost, but depreciation is not a variable expense. The monthly payment on that tractor will not change whether you pick up and deliver 10 shipments or 20 shipments on a given day. It remains the same. The bank could care less whether you use that tractor or not; it just wants its monthly payment. Similarly, salaries of terminal managers and salespeople can be considered a direct cost or fixed cost, but they do not vary. Those costs will not change with a change in volume or output. However, a P&D driver picking up a shipment with 5 pieces has a different cost than a driver picking up a shipment with 40 pieces. The time to handle the two shipments is different and cost varies with each piece on a one-to-one basis.

The first step is understanding costs and how they behave with a change in volume or output. The variable/fixed income statement is the vehicle for that understanding.

Step 2: Identify the company's stage in the business cycle: trauma, stabilization, or return to growth.
It is important to understand that a company can be a managerial or economic failure long before it becomes a failure in the legal sense if it continues to be able to meet its current financial obligations. The earlier you catch a decline, the easier it is to extract the company from that situation. The longer you allow the decline to continue, the more difficult and expensive to arrest the decline and turn it around.

What should we be looking for?

Cash position! Cash is king! If you're bleeding cash and cannot meet your current financial obligations and your balance sheet is waterlogged, you're in the trauma stage. How early you realize that and react to it determines the likelihood of your company's survival.

Along with understanding your cash position, trend your variable cost as a percent of revenue or sales. If it is trending toward the 70% number, or above that number, you've got problems. You're probably seeing your contribution margin and contribution dollars to cover fixed costs and overhead declining.

Trend your revenue per shipment, variable cost per shipment, and contribution dollars per shipment. The bottom line is that if your contribution dollars per shipment figure is declining, you must handle more shipments to generate the contribution dollars needed to cover fixed cost and overhead. If you don't understand your cost, this is where the vicious cycle begins. If your contribution dollars per shipment figure is declining, the quality of revenue is declining or variable cost per shipment is increasing, or it could be a combination of both. Use that relationship as one of your early warning signs.

Another key area to watch is the percent of revenue growth and percent of shipment count growth. For example, I just did an analysis of a company that was stagnant and poised to begin declining. Over the last two years revenue growth was 5.96% and shipment count growth was 11.78%. Variable cost in dollars and in percentage was growing because the quality of revenue was declining, and operations, due to the productivity methods used, was throwing more people and equipment at the problem. Watch your revenue, variable cost, and contribution dollars per shipment relationship. That can tell you a whole lot about what is happening in your organization.

Ask yourself, "Has my company plateaued from a growth and or profitability standpoint"? It is acceptable for a company to plateau or pause for a brief period of time to gain new direction. However, an extended plateau puts the company at risk. I consider nine months to a year for an LTL carrier (depending on the size of the company) to be the maximum acceptable plateau period.

When a company plateaus it has three options:

1.   It can do nothing and wait for some business hazard to come along and sink it.

2.   It can implement strong profit-improvement programs.

3.   It can sell off losing assets and regroup.

One thing is certain; if a company does not choose one of the latter two options it will fail. If you choose the second option, I suggest you go back and read Chapter 3 on the barrier of complexity. Selecting the second option means a change in culture.

Understand the game to make sure you're treating the company's problems, not the symptoms.

Step 3: Implement the TPG cost model that has the capability to measure capacity and capacity utilization in pickup and delivery, dock and linehaul trailer utilization.

Measuring capacity and capacity utilization in P&D is difficult to do because there are so many variables. It's relatively easy to measure capacity in linehaul, isn't it? You simply inspect the linehaul trailer visually and note the weight of the trailer and you can determine if the trailer is at 70% capacity or 60% capacity.

In P&D, it's simply not that easy. You can't look at a P&D trailer and determine capacity and capacity utilization. Now, you might look at the trailer and say, "It's got 26 skids on it," or, "It is 80% full from a visual standpoint," but that doesn't mean that unit is full from a capacity and productivity standpoint. There are many variables that must be quantified to determine capacity and utilization on a P&D run. For example, how many miles is the P&D trip: 100 or 300? A driver who has to drive 300 miles does not have the time to do as much work as a driver who only drives 100 miles. Thus, capacity is different for those two runs. How many hours does the driver work in a day? A driver working 11 hours needs a different workload than a driver working 7 hours. In what geographic area is the trip? It takes longer to drive 100 miles in Philadelphia than it does in Hazleton, PA.

Length of the trip, driver workload, and geography are a few of the variables that must be quantified in order to determine the capacity or capacity utilization of a P&D run and P&D operation within a terminal.

If a carrier can't measure capacity and capacity utilization in P&D, it cannot know its true cost and will not know how much additional work (which brings revenue with it) it can absorb in the terminal and company. As we discussed in earlier chapters, one of the major keys to building long-term, sustainable profitability in an LTL carrier is growing revenue and absorbing that revenue with capacity already in place. That is how you build operating leverage into the company.

We operate in a world of constraints. You must know the mileage and geography of a trip to determine the time it should take to complete the trip. Each shipment is different, so you must know the time it takes to load or unload each shipment at a customer's location based on making the stop, handling the paperwork, and handling the pieces (or handling units) of the shipment. What is the weight of the shipment? What is the density of the shipment? How long will it take to unload given the weight and density? If you cannot determine the time requirement for all of the above variables, you will find yourself over-costing, under-costing, and occasionally, due to pure luck, costing a shipment correctly. Not very comforting, is it?

By determining the operational capacity of a terminal, real and measurable sales goals can be developed. This also gives the terminal and the company an understanding of how much additional business they can handle without adding any additional cost in the P&D, dock, and linehaul operations.

Sales and Capacity

First, traditional systems assume the P&D operation is at 100% capacity. In my 33 years in the LTL industry, I have yet to see in my initial analysis a P&D operation that did not have a minimum of 35% available capacity. Traditional cost models cannot measure capacity and capacity utilization, so they are not able to factor into the costing and pricing process the value of that excess capacity to the company. Simply put, companies tend to over-cost potential new business and cost themselves out of market share. Also, in traditional cost models, too much cost is assigned to current business so that the carrier cannot accurately evaluate the value of a particular customer to the company.

```
                              P&D TRIP DETAIL - SUMMARY              RUN TIME 10:15:34
                          11/09/2014 THRU 11/16/2014

        COST               --------ALLOWANCE--------  -PERFORMANCE- --------LTL------- ---------TL-------- -----LTL SPOTS----- TL
DATE AREA NET DELY MILES PKUP  DLVR  PRWK  TOTAL   DRV  MGT ST SH  HU  WEIGHT ST SH HU  WEIGHT ST SH  HU WEIGHT SF

TAM TOTALS   1 -
 1    1,420.33          270.13          1,312.33       2,110   3,717,290        0       1,201              3
 2       31.75                 260.50               92.40   3,170                0          0   2,362
 3           24,916                530.63              121.25   8,157          0           94          952,428
 8   MILES/STOP: 11.3  SB TRIPS:        137.60   RETS/TRIP:   .6       MISPCK/TRIP:   .0

3RD TOT
 1    1,420.33          270.13          1,312.33       2,110   3,717,290        0       1,201              3
 2       31.75                 260.50               92.40   3,170                0          0   2,362
 3           24,916                530.63              121.25   8,157          0           94          952,428

TRIPS:    168 MILES/TRIP: 149   MILES/STOP: 11.3  SB TRIPS:     137.60   RETS/TRIP:   .6       MISPCK/TRIP:   .3
```

Measuring capacity helps in setting realistic sales goals, as noted above. In the diagram above under the performance section you see two columns: DRV and MGT. The important column is the MGT column. This measures the capacity a terminal/company has in the pickup and delivery operation. In this example, the number is 121.25. This means the terminal has the ability to handle 21.25 percent more work with its current trucks and drivers.

The method I use is focused on the LTL shipments. Notice the terminal handled 3,170 LTL shipments that week in P&D. By taking the 3,170 shipments and multiplying that by 1.2125, we see that the terminal can handle 3,970 shipments with cost and capacity already in place. Taking the difference between the two numbers, 3,970 and 3,170, we see that 800 more shipments a week could be handled in that terminal. If we divide that by 5 days that comes to an additional 160 shipments a day. Now that sounds like an insurmountable task, but let's break it down. The terminal ran 168 pickup and delivery trips for the week, or 34 trips a day. If we take 160 and divide it by 34, that is an additional 5 shipments per pickup and delivery trip. The terminal is averaging 1.5 shipments per stop, so if you take 5 and divide by 1.5, that would equate to 3 additional stops per trip.

Now, not every trip would have an additional three stops; some might not have any additional stops, but some might have one or two more. You spread the additional work over a multitude of pickup and delivery trips. Let me pose this questions to you. Would you take two additional shipments per trip with the same costs? If the terminal is averaging $120.00 revenue per shipment and you add $240.00 additional revenue per pickup and delivery run, with no additional cost, would you take that? Can you imagine the impact on profitability and lower cost? Grow and absorb with capacity already in place—it's powerful stuff!

Step 4: Generate revenue growth using the TPG capacity-based costing model that factors in non-related costs and the value of unused capacity.

There are costs that are not related to picking up shipments, delivering shipments, or working freight across a dock. Although they are variable because they are included in wages for P&D and dockworkers, they are not variable on a one-to-one basis in providing those services.

Take a look at the chart below. Customer delay in a pickup and delivery operation is a legitimate expense in P&D. However, not every customer causes the drivers a delay while picking up and delivering freight. If you do not remove that time from variable cost in P&D, you're adding too much variable cost when costing a customer's business. You're also making all customers pay for those customers that cause a delay, which is not fair. In the example below, the company had 1,886.45 hours of delay time in P&D for the month at a cost of $57,009.

There are other non-related costs a P&D driver incurs at times that do not vary on a one-to-one basis when picking up or delivering a shipment. Examples include equipment failure, random drug screens, and a driver performing leadman work. You might think you should allocate them across the P&D operation, but every shipment is different, and every P&D run is different. What then should be your basis of allocation?

Notice in the exhibit that the company reports 17,784 hours of dock inefficiencies and $249,208 dollars of P&D inefficiencies. Are our operating inefficiencies the customers' fault? In some cases yes, but in all cases? No. A carrier's inefficiencies in P&D and dock belong to the carrier. If you cannot quantify those inefficiencies and remove them from variable cost, you just added too much variable cost to your costing process and you reduced market share available to your company. Effectively, you are over-costing your business. A carrier's operating inefficiencies belong to the carrier and shouldn't be passed on to all customers in the form of higher prices. If you know of customers that do cause inefficiencies, make those customers pay for their inefficiencies, not all of your customers.

In the P&D example above, we saw that this particular terminal had 21.25% of its P&D cost tied up in inefficiencies. If you add inefficiencies to your P&D variable cost in the costing process, you have assigned too much cost to the customer and you will not know the true quality of a customer's business.

Non- Related Costs		
Excluded	0.00	$ -
Linehaul	0.00	$ -
Driver Dock	642.71	$ 19,423
P&D Admin	122.30	$ 3,696
Customer Delay	1,886.45	$ 57,009
Total Non-Related	2,651.46	$ 80,127
Dock Inefficiencies	588.50	17,784
P&D Inefficiencies	0.00	$ 249,208
Variable Cost Reduced	$ 347,120	

In the exhibit above, the carrier has $347,120 of non-related costs and operating inefficiencies for the month. If the carrier leaves that cost in variable cost during the costing process, it just left a lot of business it should be handling in the marketplace because it costed itself out of that business. Without those costs removed, it is impossible to evaluate the true value of a customer's business to the company. By removing those costs, the carrier adds in the value of unused capacity to the company.

Again, all other costing systems assume the carrier is operating at 100% capacity and that, in my experience, is just not true. Furthermore, the P&L statement has all the non-related costs and operating inefficiencies included in the numbers. You must be able to quantify and remove those costs from variable cost if you're going to properly cost customers.

If you cannot measure capacity and capacity utilization in pickup and delivery, dock/platform and linehaul trailer utilization, you do not know your true costs. Thus, you're leaving market share that you should be handling available to competitors because you're adding too much variable cost to the costing process. You're not factoring in the potential value of unused capacity to the company. Your costing system must have that capability.

Step 5: Absorb revenue growth with cost and capacity already in place.

Step 6: Measure management and supervision at the terminal level in controlling cost and absorbing revenue growth in the pickup and delivery, dock, and linehaul trailer utilization with current capacity in place.

We can combine steps 5 and 6. Carriers need to absorb growth with capacity in place and must measure management and supervision at the terminal level to make certain that is happening and that they are not throwing more cost at the growth.

Let's take another look at the P&D report above that we used to determine the sales volume that could be handled without adding cost to the pickup and delivery operation.

```
                                         P&D TRIP DETAIL - SUMMARY              RUN TIME 10:15:34
                                     11/09/2014 THRU 11/16/2014

        COST            --------ALLOWANCE--------  -PERFORMANCE- --------LTL--------  ---------TL-------- -----LTL SPOTS----- TI
   DATE AREA NET DELY MILES PKUP  DLVR  PRWK  TOTAL  DRV  MGT ST SH  HU  WEIGHT ST SH  HU  WEIGHT ST SH  HU  WEIGHT SE

   TRM TOTALS   1 -
   S1   1,420.33          270.13      1,312.33       2,110   3,717,290          0          1,201
   S2      31.75   260.50            92.40   3,170          0          0  2,360
   S3      24,916          530.63      121.25  8,157          0          94   952,428

   S  MILES/STOP: 11.3  SB TRIPS:     137.60  RETS/TRIP:   .6        MISPCK/TRIP:  .0 -----------------------------

   SRD TOT
   S1   1,420.33          270.13      1,312.33       2,110   3,717,290          0          1,201
   S2      31.75   260.50            92.40   3,170          0          0  2,360
   S3      24,916          530.63      121.25  8,157          0          94   952,428

   TRIPS:    168  MILES/TRIP: 148  MILES/STOP: 11.3  SB TRIPS:    137.60  RETS/TRIP:  .6        MISPCK/TRIP:  .0
```

As revenue and shipment count grows, it is vital that the terminals and company absorb that growth with current capacity and cost because absorbing with capacity already in place builds operating leverage, reduces variable cost per shipment, and improves profitability. The key number to look for is what we call the ratio of PRWK (productive work) to net hours (time the driver is on the street performing P&D work).

Please notice the column labeled PRWK. The system uses engineered standards in P&D for stops, shipment handling units (pieces), and weight. There are standards for

LTL, TL (truckload), LTL Drop and Pick (dropping off or picking up a trailer with LTL shipments at a customer's dock), and TL Spot (dropping off or picking up a truckload at a customer's dock). Each shipment has a different time, and therefore cost. So the TPG system calculates the time allowed to handle each shipment in hours.

In the terminal above, the number calculated by the system was 530.63 hours. Now notice the column showing net hours. The drivers were on the street 1,420.33 hours that week. If we take the 560.63 hours of productive work and divide that number by the net hours we will get the percent of the driver's day doing productive work. In the example above, that number is .3736, or 37.36%. The remaining 62.37% was used doing the pre- and post-trip inspection and driving the 148 miles.

Obviously the carrier wants the 37.36% to improve. The MGT number of 121.25 shows that the P&D cost is 21.25% higher than it should be, or that the carrier has the capacity to do 21.25% additional work with the cost already in place. So, as the sales team increases revenue and shipment count, we should see the total PRWK number increase. The key statement follows. If the terminal is absorbing the additional work, the 37.36% should increase and the 121.25 MGT (management performance) number should become lower, moving toward the standard of 100. That number is perfect.

If we see PRWK increasing, the 37.36% failing to improve, and the MGT number increasing, the terminal is not absorbing, but instead adding cost to the P&D operation. Not what you want to see. The same logic holds true with dock productivity and linehaul trailer utilization.

Measure capacity and capacity utilization in those three key operating areas and absorb growth with capacity and cost already in place.

Step 7: Build a more productive customer base through TPG Customer Base Analysis programs by segmenting customers into contribution categories.

_The objective of customer base analysis is to make sure you're constantly improving the contribution dollars generated by your customers. In fact, I put more emphasis on what I call the "back end" of the costing and pricing process.

What I mean by that statement is information from account managers and customers is not always accurate. It's not that they are all secretly withholding information; it's just that at times the information they provide is inaccurate or incomplete.

If a pricing analysis on new business comes close, I suggest giving it a shot. Once you get some experience handling the business for 60 or 90 days, pull a customer profitability report and analyze the level of profitability. Assign people to pull customer reports and analyze them for contribution. Account managers just cannot cover all their territory and having a customer base analysis process in place allows the analyst to sort out the good, bad, and ugly and forward to the sales department.

For example, at one company I'm consulting with, we are currently working on rate increases for all customers that have a contribution ratio of 101 to 140. Once we feel comfortable we've exhausted that group, we'll move to the next bracket and work on that group. The thing to remember about a price increase is that money falls straight to the bottom line because there is no cost increase.

A company has three groups of customers. The first group includes those that are not even covering variable or out-of-pocket costs, and that wreaks havoc with the cash flow cycle. This group of customers has no value to the company whatsoever. Also, in most cases the rate increase needed to get them to some level of contribution is so large you don't have a chance of the customers accepting it. Cut them loose and you'll see cash flow improve!

The second group is what I call the "tweeners." They are covering variable or out-of-pocket cost, but are not profitable. This is the group you have to be really careful with. Companies that use operating ratio as the basis of determining the value of a customer to the company get in trouble here. A customer can have an operating ratio of 106 and not be profitable.

In many "tweener" cases a carrier will try to get a rate increase and if not, they cut the client loose. You just hurt your company. Though they are not profitable, they are generating contribution dollars to cover fixed cost and overhead and if you cut them loose you just made the situation worse. You should endeavor, through customer-base analysis, to get rate increases on this segment to generate a higher level of contribution to the company. Tread carefully here!

The third segment is the profitable group! These are the customers that are profitable and your job here is to protect them and not lose them to the competition. This is the segment you want to grow.

The objective is to reduce the percentage of customers that are not covering variable cost, seek out rate increases on the group that is not profitable, but generating contribution dollars, and protect, with all your might, the profitable group!

What I generally find is the first group is around 5 to 7%, the second group is in the 20 to 25% range, and the third group is in the 70 to 75% range.

It is important to understand your customer base's impact on profitability.

Step 8: Put everyone in the company on the same page by implementing the TPG performance-based incentive compensation program.
The majority of incentive compensation programs fail primarily because of the following:

It's an all or nothing program. The numbers are hit or they're not, and if not that means no payout.
The individual's compensation is tied to areas he or she has no control over.
The payout period is too far out.

Incentive compensation is designed to reward people over and above their base compensation. The idea is to motivate employees to perform at or above the goal(s) of the organization.

Unfortunately, often the individual depends on others to be successful in areas that the individual has no direct control over. For example, a dockworker has no input whatsoever on the amount of equipment senior management decides to purchase, or the return on investment of that decision. A customer service agent has no direct control over the number of P&D drivers a terminal manager hires.

An account representative is responsible for generating profitable revenue for the company. Now, the costing and pricing department has some impact on that, but the account representative should have revenue goals to hit. If the account rep is finding profitable revenue opportunities, costing and pricing will give approval. So, perhaps the account representative should have their incentive compensation as follows. Perhaps 25% should be tied to the terminal revenue goal, and 75% tied to the account rep's territory goal. Let's take a look at how this would work.

Account Revenue Achievment	
Acct Rep	
Per Cent of	% Of Points
Budget Achiev.	Earned
97.75%	10.00%
98.00%	20.00%
98.25%	30.00%
98.50%	40.00%
98.75%	50.00%
99.00%	60.00%
99.25%	70.00%
99.50%	80.00%
99.75%	90.00%
100.00%	100.00%

In the table above, if the account representative achieves 99% of the territory revenue goal he or she would receive 60% of the value that represents this category.

Terminal Revenue Achievment	
Per Cent of	% Of Points
Budget Achiev.	Earned
80.00%	10.00%
82.00%	20.00%
84.00%	30.00%
86.00%	40.00%
88.00%	50.00%
90.00%	60.00%
92.00%	70.00%
95.00%	80.00%
97.50%	90.00%
100.00%	100.00%

In the table above, if the terminal achieves 90.0%, the account reps would receive 60% of the value that represents that category.

This keeps the account representative motivated because some level of compensation will be received. It's not an all-or-nothing situation.

An inbound front-line supervisor might have their compensation tied to the following: 25% to on-time delivery performance, 25% to loss and damage claims, 25% to pickup and delivery management performance and 25% to inbound dock efficiency. Using a similar method as the charts above, it is not an all-or-nothing scenario.

The outbound supervisor might have their compensation tied to the following: 25% to on-time linehaul cuts, 25% loss and damage, 25% to outbound linehaul trailer utilization percentage, and 25% to outbound dock efficiency.

In my opinion, a terminal or service center manager's compensation should be tied to two areas. A terminal manager is responsible for terminal revenue growth and terminal profitability. So while tied to a percentage table similar to the ones exhibited here, 50% of his or her incentive is tied to terminal revenue growth and 50% to terminal profitability.

Every person in the company should be eligible for performance-based compensation, all the wat to the janitor. However, payout should be based as closely as possible on areas employees have direct control over, and it should not be an all-or-nothing program. The idea is to keep everyone on the same page by rewarding them for continuous improvement in the areas they have control over that, collectively, will improve performance and profitability for the entire organization.

Compensation payout should be awarded as close in time to the performance as possible. Having a payout once a year just doesn't cut it. Too far in the future and a bad quarter could wreck the entire year, negating any hopeful motivation to succeed. I suggest incentive compensation be paid at least quarterly, if not monthly.

The TPG incentive program is much too detailed to fully explain in this book. However, a good incentive program will give the individual a chance to win and the opportunity to receive some level of payout, keeping them motivated to help the company reach its goals. It should not be an all-or-nothing program. Get everyone on the same page by tying compensation to the areas they have control over.

The LTL Carrier's Profitability Blueprint

SUMMARY

Well, the journey is complete. I truly hope you found the book helpful and discovered some ideas, concepts, and plans that inspired you. I have thoroughly enjoyed writing it for you. Believe me, it has been a labor of love! My passion is coaching, teaching, and sharing knowledge.

I would like to leave you with several main points to remember. First, make the personal commitment to continue to learn and grow so you can continue to achieve at a high level. The operating environment is always moving to a higher, more complex level. Don't get left behind!

Second, remember that in order to understand your cost, you must know the capacity of your pickup and delivery operation and dock operation, and the percent of utilization. As we have discussed, linehaul capacity is pretty easy to understand. Pickup and delivery and dock is much more complex. Your costing system must have the capability to factor in the value of unused capacity in the costing process.

Next, be aware of some early warning signals for your company. Make it a habit to look at several key figures and analyze them on a monthly basis. One I definitely recommend is breakeven revenue and shipment count. Don't fall into the trap of chasing expenses with revenue for revenue's sake. It's a vicious cycle and the chances of success are small; many companies have been put out of business with that flawed thinking. If you follow the Blueprint you will be able to determine the problem instead of treating the symptom. If you do not understand the breakeven calculation, please reach out to me and I will help you get through the box and understand it. An LTL carrier is so capital intense that understanding this calculation is critical. As noted in the book, a 1% change in variable cost will drive a 3 to 7% change in breakeven, in either the up or down direction. Watch your revenue, variable cost, and contribution dollars per shipment figures as well for early warning signs of trouble.

In every carrier I have worked with that was in the decline stage, the problem, without exception, has been the relationship of variable cost to revenue. So many consultants attack fixed cost because that is easy to understand and because they do not understand the complexity that makes up variable cost in an LTL carrier. You can cut fixed cost once, maybe twice, but then what do you do? You've treated the symptom, not the problem. Within a couple of months the company will be right back where it was before the cuts: decline! I tell clients that if fixed cost and overhead is the reason for decline, they should go out of business. Never, in my career, have I found that to be the case.

Remember that a carrier, or any company for that matter, has three kinds of resources at hand: human, financial, and physical. I have found that the quality of the human resources determines the level of financial resources, which determines the quality and quantity of your physical resources. Leadership—it's all you've got! Just like a sports team does, make certain you take advantage of every chance you have to trade up when replacing someone. Build a team of four- and five-star players and coaches. It is through people that performance of any kind, good or bad, is posted. Always trade up when the opportunity arises.

Also, a company must grow! Running a company is like riding a bicycle: You either keep moving forward or you fall down. Growth is one of the universal laws, both personally and from a business standpoint. A company can pause for a brief time to get its bearings, but it must grow or it will enter decline.

I love leaders! Leaders are so courageous, such gutsy people! Tony Robbins said it better than I could ever communicate when it comes to life and running a business. He said, "Life is like swimming in the ocean, if a wave isn't knocking you down now, don't worry one is on the way." Isn't that so true? I have found that each time you get knocked down you have a decision to make. Either get up and keep swimming, or quit! There is no in between. In my career I have run across what I would describe as two types of leaders. The first type sits around thinking about how not to lose money. The second type sits around thinking about how to make money!

Those who know me would tell you I could go on and on (and probably do more than I should at times), but as we used to say as coaches, it's time to tee it up and hit someone! During the off-season so much recruiting, preparation, and practice takes place that by the time the first game approaches, players and coaches just want to play! I believe that's where we are in our journey. You've read the book; now begin implementing what you've learned.

Best wishes for a happy, successful life!

INDEX

Page locators with a t at the end refer to tables on the page.
Bolded numbers indicate a definition.

A

ABC (activity-based costing), 98–99
accountability, 10, 12
accounting system, 10–12, 16
accounts receivable, 7
acquisition
  failure of, 96
  growth through, 13, 15, 94
assets/reduction of, 5, 121

B

back-to-growth
  long-term, 13
  potential, 9
  sales, marketing strategy, 15
  strategy, 6, 13
barrier of complexity
  adjusting to the, 35, 45–46
  by thrashabout, 6, 10, 35, 50, 67, 105, 119
  carrier categories, 36–38
  competitive advantage, 47
  competitive edge and, 42
  culture and, 36
  goals and, 43, 101
  Groundhog Day, 35
  leadership and, 39, 41–43, 67
  management by thrashabout, 6, 10, 35, 50, 67, 105, 119
  operating measurements and, 9
  profit improvement program, 5
bills per
  measurement by, 48, 61–62, 61t, 62t
  profitability of, 61, 61t, 62, 62t
bleeding, 11

blueprint
  begin at the end, 59
  eight steps of, 118
  measure capacity/capacity utilization, 59
  profitability, 1, 15, 132
  strategy, goals, execution, 106
  summary, 132
bonuses, 79
breakeven (break even)
  calculating, 29–30, 32t, 33, 33t, 132
  contribution margin and, 26
  contribution ratio and, 72
  CVC (cost, volume, contribution), 27
  declining, 4, 28–29
  how to reach, 16–17, 72, 119
  per day numbers, 32–33, 33t
  relationships, 27
  revenue, 29–30, 32–33, 33t
  stabilization stage, 9
  trauma stage, 28–30
  treating symptoms, 19
  trend of, 20
  variable cost fluctuations and, 32–33, 32t, 33t, 119
Bryant, Coach Bear, 79, 105
Bucket List, 70–73, 72t, 73t
business cycle, 6, 117–118, 120

C

calculations
  basic unit costs, 117
  breakeven and, 20
  incentive, 87

linehaul measurements, 61–63,
    61**t,** 62**t,** 63**t**
P&D capacity, 48, 53, 124
TPG system, 127
wages, fringes, 21
capacity
    already in place, 15, 28, 31, 33,
        49–50, 55, 59, 118, 122, 124,
        126
    based costing model, 106
    breakeven point and, 33
    constraints and, 50
    cost and, 49, 51, 101, 126
    defined, 98
    dock and linehaul, 31, 48, 122
    dynamic leader, 43
    for growth, 13
    human resources, 12–14
    management, 12, 48, 126
    measurement, 16, 19–20, 28, 31,
        34, 48–50, 49**t,** 54, 98, 118,
        122–123, 123**t**
    operational, 12, 14–16, 20, 28,
        50–52, 51**t,** 54, 123, 126
    operations department and, 8
    P&D (pickup and delivery),
    pricing and, 55, 57
    profitability and, 31
    sales and, 123
    terminal, 55, 123, 123**t**
    The Formula and, 55
        throughput, 66
        unused, 124
        utilization, 8, 12, 14–16,
        19–20, 31, 33, 48, 51, 55, 66,
        99–100, 107, 117
        variable cost related to, 27–33,
        32**t,** 33**t,** 107
capital
    expenditures, 19
    growth position, 13
    investments, 2, 9, 14, 81, 99

working, 7
capital-intense
    critical calculation, 132
    customer service and, 98
    dock and linehaul, 67
    P&D capacity, 18, 67, 132
    variable costs and, 4, 16
carrier health
    buckets, 17–18, 18**t**
    categories, 36–38
    comparison, 56**t,** 69
    human resources and, 3
    market position/financial
        position, 3, 36–37, 37**t**
    minimum shipments and, 76
    next-day, two-day, 48, 56, 60
    not 100% capacity, 51–52, 54, 68,
        98, 123, 125
    percentage of variable cost to
        revenue, 17
    physical resources, 3
    regional, 31, 48, 55, 60, 64, 100,
        117
    stages, 2, 6–9, 18–19
    strategy, 19
    Type 1, Type 2, 36
    variable costs and, 17–19, 18**t,**
        27–28
cash
    bleeding, 11, 119–120
    breakeven, 71
    customer base and, 69
    flow (position), 2, 3, 5–6, 9, 11,
        18, 72, 105, 120, 128
    lending, 119
    manage, 9
    negative flow, 72, 105
    outstanding, 7
    position, 3, 5, 120
    reserves, 13
catch-22, 8
CBC (capacity-based costing),

99–100, 106, 118, 124

change

constant, 105

    decline and failure, 1–2

    embrace, 117

    in culture, 5, 36, 121

    management styles and, 41–42

    pain increases to, 35

    refusing to, 6

    to customer base, 8

claims, 12, 16, 24, 25**t**, 26, 92, 131

communication

    confidentiality of, 89

    line of, 13

    of goals, 95

    with management, 13

    within management team, 10

compensation

    incentive, 79–81, 87, 129–130, 130**t**

    payout, 81, 87, 129, 131

    plan, 91–93, 95, 97

    The Formula, 118

    TPG incentive, 129–131

    workers, 21, 22**t**

competitive

    advantage, 40, 42, 47, 98, 100–101, 103

    disadvantage, 6

    edge, 42

complexity barrier *See barrier of complexity*

constraints, 50, 57, 59, 62, 67, 122

consulting

    modus operandi, 71

    real life case, 95–97, 128

contribution dollars

    and variable cost, 18–19, 18**t**, 27–29, 119

    bottom line, 121

    customer base and, 7–8, 72–76, 72**t**, 73**t**, 127–128

divided by revenue, 26, 29

increased, 15

per day numbers, 33**t**

per shipment in CVC, 20, 76

relationships per shipment, 4, 20, 26–27, 29, 33, 70–73, 121

stabilization stage strategy, 15

to cover fixed costs, 4, 18–19, 18**t**, 120–121

warning signs, 121, 132

control

    capacity, 8

    cost measurements, 19, 29, 49–50

    defects, 38

    outdated cost, 19, 49–50, 49**t**

    profitability, 31

    systems, 9–11

    through stabilization stage, 10

    variable cost, 27, 29

cost

    ABC (activity-based costing), 98–99

    billing and collecting, 24, 24**t**

    breakdowns, 12

    categories of variable, 25

    CBC (capacity-based costing), 99–100

    change in output and, 8, 16, 18, 120

    delivery, 51–52, 51**t**

    depreciation, 18–19, 23, 26, 120

    direct, 7, 18, 73, 78

    equipment, 7, 12, 18, 23, 25–26, 53, 64, 93, 99

    fallacies in costing P&D, 51

    fixed, 4, 8, 18–19, 26–30, 33, 33**t**, 67, 72–75, 100, 107, 120–121

    fringe, 12, 20–21, 23–26, 59, 64, 117

    fundamentals of, 99–100

    labor, 53

    linehaul lane balance, 63–64

models, 6, 51–52, 98–99, 123
non-related, 124–125, 125**t**
P&D, 9, 20–21, 25, 51–53, 53**t,**
    55–57, 56**t**
P&D (pickup & delivery) driver,
    22**t**
per day numbers, 33, 33**t**
per mile, 21, 23, 24**t**, 25, 52–53,
    56**t**, 57, 64
per shipment, 65
reduce, 8
semi-fixed, 26–27, 120
systems, 18, 20–21, 31, 51, 67, 95,
    98–99, 125
tariff based, 26, 101
The Formula, 55, 118–132
transaction level, 99
understand, 2, 16, 31, 50, 69,
    98–99, 101, 116–117,
    119–121, 132
variable, 4, **7,** 8–9, 15–19, 17**t,**
    18**t**, 25–33, 25**t**, 33**t**, 67, 70,
    72**t**, 73–74, 73**t**, 74**t**, 107,
    116–117, 124–125
crossdock, 65–66
cube (space)
    fundamentals of, 99
    linehaul, 50, 62–63, 67, 70
culture
    "barrier of complexity," 5
    adjusting, 46
    blending, 96
    change, 5, 14, 36, 58, 121
    improved, 10
    of accountability, 10
customer
    base, 3, 7–8, 12, 69, 73, 73**t**, 75,
        77, 100, 117–118, 127–128
    Base Analysis program, 71, 118,
        127–128
    Bucket List, 70–73
    build, 118

categories, 118, 127–128
CBC (capacity-based costing),
    99–100
contribution dollars, 127
cost, 125, 125**t**
delay, 124–125, 125**t**
operating ratio of, 128
profitability, 7, 12, 51, 70, 70**t,**
    72–75, 74**t**, 75**t**, 123,
    128–129
relationships, 100
segmentation, 73**t**, 74–78, 74**t,**
    75**t**
selective retention, 15, 72–75, 128
service, 14, 40
special handling for, 69
tweeners, 128
volume, 100
weight breaks, 69
CVC(cost, volume,contribution), 16,
    20, 27–29, 31

D
decline and failure
    company, 1, 5, 15, 72, 105, 119
    internal/external forces, 2–4
    variable cost to revenue
        relationship, 132
delivery, 51–52
density (pounds per cubic feet) PCF
    and efficiency, 61
    customer setup of, 69
    dim weight or, 69
    freight, 57
    shipment, 50, 65, 122
depreciation, 18–19, 23, 26, 120
deregulation, 1
dim weight, 69
Dinosaur, 36–38, 37**t**, 47
dispatch, 57–58, 60, 62, 67
dock and platform

capacity, 28, 31, 59, 66, 107, 116, 122–123, 132
costs, 12, 21, 59, 64, 66, 73, 116
crossdock time and, 65–66
efficiencies, 65
freight, 65, 99
inbound/outbound, 65–66, 99
inefficiencies, 124–125, 125**t**
linehaul measurements, 60–64
live load/unload, 66
management of, 12, 16, 19–20, 59, 64, 126
methodology, 65–66
operations, 14, 59, 64–67
physical size, 65, 99
productivity, 65–66, 127
profitability, 59
queue, 16, 59
The Formula and, 118
time allowances and, 63, 66, 99–100
variable costs management of, 16, 25, 107
dock/platform workers, 21
Drucker, Peter, 48, 117
DRV, 123
Durant, Will and Ariel, 1

E
Eagle, 36–38, 37**t**, 40, 47
EBITDA(earnings before interest, taxes, depreciation and amortization), 11
employees
job code, 84, 84**t**, 91–92
manage, 13, 40, 81, 102–103, 117, 129
payout to, 81, 89, 131
retention of, 104
the right, 103
equipment
cost, 12, 26, 53, 99

depreciation, 18–19, 23, 26, 120
failure/expense, 93, 124
maintenance of, 7
expenses
breakdowns, 12, 22**t**
breakeven, 29–30
business, 26
customer delay, 124, 125**t**
increased, 30
mechanic wages, fringes, 25
mileage, 21, 23, 24**t,** 25
operating, 87
semi-fixed percents, 17
towing, tires, tubes, 23
trucking, 23, 24**t,** 25

F
factors
cube, 99
distance, 99
geography, 50
handling units, 65
inbound/outbound, 99
linehaul lane balance, 63–64, 63**t,** 99
sort and seg, 99
time, 100–101
weight, 99
fixed
contribution dollars per shipment, 4, 28, 72–75, 100, 107, 120–121, 128
cost, 4, 7–8, 16–19, 17**t**, 18**t**, 23, 26–30, 33**t**, 67, 72–75, 100, 107, 120–121, 132
semi-, 26–27, 73
football comparisons, 9–11, 14, 34, 58, 68, 94, 102, 106, 110–116, 119
Formula: Building Competitive Advantage, 5, 35
freight
bill, 24, 24**t,** 26

constraints, 50, 57, 59, 62–63, 67, 122

delays, 124

density, 57, 61

inbound/outbound, 65–66, 99

inbound/outbound, 61

load avg, 60, 64–67

65–66, 99

WK (productive work), 54

revenue, 25

sort-and-segment (sort and seg), 66, 99

special handling of, 69

weight per shipment, 61

FSC (fuel surcharge), 20, 21, 23, 25

fundamentals

    communication, 46

    enduring, 9, 16, 34, 68, 117

    measuring, 99–100

    of profitability

G

geography

    capacity utilization and, 48

    P&D constraints, 50, 122

goals

    accurate capacity measurement to, 50

    growth and, 43–45, 98

    plan together, 10, 105

    program, 110

    revenue, 55, 129

    sales, 50, 123

    silo methodology of, 79

    specific, 14

    strategic objectives and, 95, 102, 106

Grisanti, Frank, 36

Groundhog Day, 35

growth

    absorb revenue, 118, 126

back to growth, 2, 6, 9, 13, 15

barrier of complexity and, 5, 42, 46–47

bottom line and, 94

capacity and, 99–100

customer-base, 100

goals and, 98

human capacity and, 13

or decline, 94, 105, 133

performance and, 13

personal, 42–43, 45–46, 102, 116

plateau, 5, 121

relationship between revenue and shipment, 4, 27, 119, 121

revenue, increase, 15, 55, 124, 131

sales, 4, 14

strategy, 95, 119

success and, 94

The Formula and, 55, 118

through acquisition, 13, 15, 94

growth-for-growth's sake, 5, 8, 19, 27, 94

H

handling units, 65

Hawk, 36–38, 37**t,** 47

headhaul lane, 63–64

human resources, 2–3, 14, 22t, 133

I

in the mix, 12, 19, 65–67

income statement

    costing on, 23, 26, 52

    Formula, 118

    operating, 11

    P&D at 100% on, 52

    per day numbers, 23

    traditional, 11

    understand your, 98

    variable/fixed, 8, 16, 20–21, 31, 117–120

insurance and claims (I&C)
  claims expense, 24, 26
  medical, 21
  PL/PD (property liability and
    property damage), 16, 21, 24,
    26
  worker's compensation, 21
interline/partner payout, 20, 25
investment
  and fixed cost, 18
  capital, 2, 9, 14, 81, 99
  compensation and, 81
  lenders about, 119
  re-, 87
  return on, 2, 67–68
  strategy of, 99
invisible problems, 6, 19, 67, 104
ITFA, 24t
ITFA tax (International Fuel Tax
  Agreement), 24t

K
Kami, Michael J., and Ross, Joel E., 94

L
leaders/leadership
  blueprint for, 35
  bottom line and, 4, 39
  bureaucratic, 41–42
  cannot see the problem, 19, 67
  categories of, 36–38, 37t
  challenge of change, 1, 3, 9,
    35–36, 46
  commitments of, 1, 35–36, 41, 46,
    54, 102–103, 116, 118
  expertise, 2, 42–43, 45
  future-oriented, 39, 42
  growth of, 46, 69, 102, 118
  healthy, weak, 1, 3, 37, 37t, 39
  market leaders, 3, 38–41, 47, 59,
    116

  poor performance, 27, 37–39, 45,
    94
  problems and, 5, 19–35
  strategy and, 102, 105
  success and, 1–4, 15, 45, 100
  vision, 87, 107
leverage
  grow revenue and, 2
  operating, 39, 49, 55, 57,
    117, 122, 126, 91
  P&D is, 55–57
  points, 56, 101, 106
linehaul trailer
  bills per, 61
  capacity, 48, 50, 62, 122, 126–127,
    126t
  cube, 50, 59, 62–63
  dock management, 9, 12, 59, 64,
    66
  efficiency, 56, 62, 64, 66
  headhaul lane, 63
  lane balance, 63, 63t
  load average, 61–62
  measurements, 60–61
  schedule of, 80
  The Formula and, 118
  utilization, 9, 14, 31, 57, 59–67,
    116–118, 122, 126–127, 126t
  variable cost and, 16
  weight per shipment, 61–63
LTL (less than truck load), 127
LTL Drop and Pick, 127

M
Machiavelli, Niccolo', 35
maintenance, 7, 23, 24t, 84, 87
management (MGT)
  barrier, 46
  bureaucratic style, 41
  by thrashabout, 6, 10, 35, 50, 67,
    105, 119

communication with, 13
failure of, 35, 67, 96
financial, 10
marketing/sales and, 13, 55
measure, 63, 118, 126
micromanaged, 64
operations, 14–15
P&D, 48, 99
performance, 53, 82, 85, 127
style changes, 41
manager
accountability of, 4, 12
incentive criteria, 131
relationships of, 45
strategy by, 10, 35, 43, 100
terminal, 9, 12, 18, 62, 81–82, 84,
131
managerial accounting, 10–12, 16, 31,
118–119
market position, 36–37, 37**t**
market share
build, 15, 54, 59, 94
lose, 51, 99, 123, 125–126
maintain, 3, 7–8
marketing, 4, 10, 12–15, 14, 94, 107
measurement systems
bills per, 48, 61–62, 65
CBC (capacity-based costing),
99–100
develop focus, 14
errors in, 67, 98
hinders profitability, 28
in the mix, 12, 19, 65–67
load average, 61
replace outdated, 6, 8–9, 28–29,
48, 65, 67
transactional complexity and, 100
medical insurance, 21
merger, 96
mileage
P&D constraints, 50, 122
per bill, 62

related expenses, 21, 23, 24**t**, 25
models
cost, 6, 51–52, 98–99, 123
TPG capacity-based costing, 20,
63, 99, 118
traditional, 51–52, 98, 123

O
objectives, 14, 79, 84, 90, 95
on-time
delivery, 14, 84
departure and arrival, 60, 80
performance, 80
operating
controls, 11
cost, 48, 51–52, 51**t**, 54, 100
efficiencies, 60, 67, 71, 75–76, 82,
100
environment, 46, 102, 132
income, 26, 33
income statement, 11
inefficiencies, 12, 70–71, 77, 116,
124–125, 125**t**
leverage, 33, 39, 49, 55, 57–58, 70,
117, 122, 126
paradigms, 9
profit and loss, 8–9
ratio, 7–8
system, 95
operating ratio
carrier comparison, 28–29,
56–57, 56**t**, 71–72
incentive goal, 80–81
measure of quality of revenue, 20
of customer, 26, 72–73, 128
to determine pricing, 8
variable cost to percent of revenue, 28–29, 73
operational capacity
human resource capacity, 13
measuring, 16, 101, 123

of terminal, 50, 67
sales and, 54
operations department
absorbs new business, 66
control capacity, 8, 107
determines variable cost, 67
efficiencies, 75–76
in stabilization stage, 14
revenue and, 52
overhead
fixed cost and, 16–17, 19, 67,
72–75, 100, 107, 120
per day, 28–30

P
P&D (pickup & delivery)
capacity measure, 28, 48–51,
53–54, 57, 63, 70, 82, 98, 107,
122, 124
capacity-based costing and, 99
carrier and, 56, 56t
classify terminals, 81–83, 82t
constraints, 50, 57, 59, 62–63, 67,
120, 122
customer delay, 124, 125t
dispatch and, 57
dock management, 64, 66
drivers, 20–21, 25, 53, 64, 81–82,
120
managing costs of, 52–53, 55–56,
56t, 64, 73, 80, 107, 127
next day, two-day, 48
operating efficiencies/inefficien-
cies, 60, 71, 125, 125t
productivity, 57, 62, 127
profitability of, 56–57, 80
PRWK, 126, 126t
relationship to time, 50, 99
schedule, 53, 60, 64, 124
stops, 54, 126, 126t
The Formula and, 58

trips, 49–50, 49t, 53, 56–57, 122
variable cost per mile, 53
zip code, 52
P&L (profit and loss statement), 28,
125
payout
bonus, 85
bucket/rules, 81–82
compensation, 21, 81–82, 87–88,
129, 130t, 131
confidential communications, 89
interline/partner, 20
job codes, 84, 84t
performance affects, 84
terminal classification, 82, 82t
PCF (pounds per cubic feet), 61, 65
per-day numbers, 23–24, 24t, 27, 33t
percent of revenue
calculating, 26, 29–30
healthy variable cost to, 17
measurements used as a, 8, 14, 19
per day numbers, 33t
profit improvement, 15
relationships, 4, 16, 17t, 18, 20, 31
shipment percent of growth to,
27, 96, 121
variable cost as, 4, 9, 15, 17–19,
18t, 26, 29–30, 33, 70, 96,
107, 116, 120
wages as, 48–49, 65
performance
based incentive compensation,
79–81, 85–93
culture of, 10
DVR (driver), 53, 123, 123t
employee commitment to, 13
leader, competitor, follower,
dropout, 36, 38
management, 82, 127
managing, 45–46
measurements, 62, 91–93, 95, 99,
123

MGT (management), 53, 123, 123**t,** 127
P&G, 80
plan, 87–93
poor, 36, 45
review, 61
reward, 81
stagnates, 42
The Formula, 118
TPG incentive, 118, 129, 130**t**
Type 2 company, 38
PL/PD (property liability & property damage), 16, 24
pricing
    capacity and, 51, 55, 66
    customer, 19, 69, 75, 97, 128
    methodology of, 8, 69, 75
    process, 123, 127
    strategy, 12, 15, 62, 77, 97
    sweet spot, 70
    to increase revenue, 15, 129
    under, 8
productivity
    dock, 65–66, 127
    improve, 13
    inaccurate measures of, 6, 14, 19–20, 28, 48, 55, 67
    manage, 9, 65, 67
    management performance and, 85, 85**t**
    methods, 121
    of customer base, 73, 78
    P&D, 48, 84, 117, 122
profitability
    blueprint for, 15, 35, 59, 118, 132
    capacity measurements and, 31, 50, 66
    capacity-based costing and, 100
    contribution dollars to fixed cost, 28
    Customer Base Analysis, 12, 72, 72**t**

customer base and, 7, 12, 15, 100, 129
CVC relationships affecting, 27–28, 76, 99
decline issues of, 28, 95, 105
foundation for, 58–59
geographic, 100
increase revenue growth, 15, 49, 122, 126
manage, 20, 67–68, 84, 98, 131
markets, customers, 12, 15, 73**t,** 74, 74**t**
minimum shipments and, 76
performance and, 13, 86
plateau, 5, 121
transaction complexity and, 100
variable cost as percent of revenue, 17–18, 18**t**, 67, 107, 116
variable/fixed income statement, 20
PRWK (productive work), 54, 126–127, 126**t**
psychology
    goals and, 40, 44
    success, 38–39
PTO (paid time off), 21

Q
queue/ dock, 59–60

R
R2A2 (recognize, relate, assimilate, apply), 107
reduce costs, 8
regulation, 6, 65
reinvest to remain, 81
relationships
    breakeven, 20, 27, 119
    capacity and cost of P&D run, 50

contribution dollars per shipment, 73, 121

customer, 100

CVC (cost, volume, contribution), 28, 31

employees, assets, 45

fixed cost/profit, 18, 18**t,** 20, 30

lender, 13

percent of revenue, 8, 14, 20, 48–49, 64–65

shipment percent of growth to revenue percent of growth, 27

variable /fixed income statement, 20, 26–28

variable cost as percent of revenue, 4, 15–17, 17**t,** 26, 29–31, 33, 107, 119, 121

variable cost-to-revenue, 18–19, 73

variable costs per shipment, 4, 16–18, 17**t,** 18**t,** 20, 27–28, 121

rent, 19, 26

repairs, 25

resources

draw off, 42

financial, 2, 5, 37, 106, 119, 133

human, 2, 3, 14, 42, 133

outside, 119

physical, 2–3, 106, 119, 133

revenue

absorb, 118, 122, 126

breakeven, 16, 20, 26–30, 119

contribution dollars divided by, 26

contribution dollars per shipment and, 15, 18–20, 28–29, 73, 76, 107, 119

CVC (cost, volume, contribution) and, 20, 27–29, 31

dollar distribution, 2–5, 30

fixed cost, 26

freight, 25

FSC (fuel surcharge), 23–24

generate, 124

growth and, 4, 9, 15, 28, 55, 76, 118, 121, 124, 131

I&C cost as percentage of revenue, 24, 26

in the mix numbers, 65

incentive achievement, 130, 130t

linehaul, P&D, 64, 126

per day numbers, 24, 32–33, 32**t,** 33**t**

per shipment, 12, 20, 26–28, 30, 33, 55, 76, 119, 121

sales, 20

semi-fixed cost, 26

shipment growth and, 4, 12, 15–16, 18, 20, 27–28

sources, 20, 25

strategy, 105

taking out, 8

The Formula and, 55, 118–119

unused capacity, 124

variable cost, **16**–19, 17**t,** 25–29, 68, 119

variable cost as percent of revenue, 4, 15–20, 17**t,** 26, 28–31, 67, 70, 107, 116

wages as percent of, 8, 14, 19, 48–49, 59, 64

warning signs, 121

risk

extended plateau, 5

progress and, 9, 10, 39, 46, 51

S

salaries, 18–19, 23, 26, 120

sales

capacity-based costing, 100

commitments, 60, 94

coordinated effort, 10, 79

goals, 123, 123**t**

growth through, 7, 9, 14–15, 66, 76, 94

operational capacity and, 54–55

plateau, 5–6

revenue, 20

stagnant /declining, 4

trauma stage strategy, 15

volume, 126–127

schedule delays/costs, 60, 64, 124

semi-fixed cost, 26–27, 73, 107, 120

service

customer, 7–8, 10, 14, 40

dock and platform, 59–60

next day or two-day, 48, 56

on time, 60, 64

shipment

breakeven, 27, 33, 119, 132

capacity measurements, 48

CBC (capacity-based costing), 99–100

constraints, 50

contribution dollars per, 4, 20, 26–29, 33, 33t, 55, 70, 73, 76–77, 119, 121

costs, 49–52, 65, 68, 124

crossdocked, 66

CVC (cost, volume, contribution), 27

density, 50, 65, 122

growth, 4, 12, 29, 119, 121

handling units, 65, 126, 126t

large volume, 70

linehaul cost per, 63–64

load average per, 61

LTL, 49, 49t, 55, 127

minimum, 76

outbound/inbound, 66, 99

PCF (pounds per cubic feet), 65

percent of growth to revenue percent of growth, 27

PRWK (productive work), 126–127

revenue per, 26–28, 30, 32t, 51–52, 56t, 73, 76

schedule, 60

special handling, 69

stem mile cost to, 51

time allowances, 65, 67, 99–100, 122, 126t, 127

truckload, 49, 49t

variable cost per, 26–30, 33, 33t, 49, 55, 73, 76, 119, 126

weight per, 61–62, 65

silo environment, 9, 58, 79

SMSA (Standard Metropolitan Statistical Area), 82

sort-and-segment, 66

space (cube) constraints, 59

stabilization stage

future team, 13–14

life cycle, 6

pricing, 12

staff

build, 103

capacity of, 101

stages

growth through, 2, 15, 42, 105

identify, 118

stagnant or declining, 4

standards, shipment, 127

strategy

cost models and, 98–101

evaluation and, 104, 117

focus, 103

growth, 95–96, 117

implement, 102, 117

implement TPG cost model, 118, 122, 124

measuring levers and, 100

pricing, 101

program, 107–110

success

employees and leaders, 45, 103(3

incentive program, 80

measurements of, 88
strategy of, 103, 105–106
variable cost as percent of revenue, 107
Sullivan, R, 16, 59, 69
systems
  accounting, 11
  control, 9
  cost based, 18, 20
  costing, 14, 125
  dispatch, 67
  operational, 14
  planning, 67
  productivity, 6
  scheduled linehaul, 60
  traditional, 51, 54, 123

T
Taxes
  highway, 24t
  ITFA, 24t
terminal
  comparison of, 56–57, 56t, 61–63, 63t
  compensation, 129–131, 130t
  destination, 60
  job codes, 84, 84t, 85, 85t
  lane balance, 63
  managing, 12, 21, 50, 60–66, 95, 99, 124, 126, 126t
  operational capacity, 50, 51t, 52–53, 53t, 67, 123, 123t
  productive work (PRWK) at, 54–55
  profitability, 131
  revenue achievement, 12, 130, 130t, 131
  The Formula, 55, 118
  TPG time calculations at, 127
  zip code, 52
The Formula
  capacity utilization, 55, 57–58

compensation, 118
cost, 55, 118–132
dock and platform, 118
growth, 55, 118
implement, 118–131
linehaul trailer, 118
P&D (pickup & delivery), 58
performance, 118
revenue, 55, 118–119
The Formula- Building Competitive Advantage, 5, 35
thrashabout management, 6, 10, 35, 50, 67, 105, 119
throughput capacity, 66
time
  algorithms, 100
  allowances, 54, 57, 63, 65
  arrival/departure, 60
  compensation, 131
  consumption, 99–100, 122
  costing, 50
  linehaul, 59
  of compensation, 131
  on street, 82
  on-time, 60
TL (Truckload carrier), 69, 127
TL Spot, 127

TPG (Transportation Profitability Group)
  Customer Base Analysis, 118
  expected hours, 82
  linehaul imbalances, 63
  system calculations, 127
  unused capacity, 124
transaction
  complexity, 100
  level costing, 99
trauma phase. See trauma stage
trauma stage
  sales, marketing strategy, 15
  strategy, 2, 9–10

trend, variable cost as percent of revenue/sales, 27, 29, 120–121
truck stops, shipments, 24**t**, 49**t**
true cost
    capacity utilization, 54–55, 122, 126
    P&D capacity, 49–50
Turtles, 36–37, 37**t**, 39, 47
Type 1 carrier, Type 2 carrier, 36

U
underpricing methodology, 8
understanding the game, 16, 34, 48, 67
utilization,
    linehaul trailer, 9, 14, 16, 31,
        48–49, 49**t**, 57, 59–67,
        116–118, 122, 126–127, 126**t**
    linehaul, capacity, 8, 12, 14–16,
        19–20, 31, 33–34, 33**t**, 48–50,
        49**t**, 54, 62, 62**t**

V
variable cost
    as percent of revenue, 17, 70, 73,
        107, 116
    blueprint, as percent of revenue,
        116
    customer and, 7–8
    fluctuations, breakeven, 32–33,
        32**t**, 33**t**
    inefficiencies and, 125
    negative/positive revenue, 31, 32**t**
    per day numbers, 33, 33**t**
    per mile, 21
    per shipment, 27, 121
    relation as percent of sales, 4
    revenue, 25–26
    sources of, 17, 17**t**
vision, 87, 107
volume, 17–18, 20

W
wages
    breakdowns, 22**t**
    dock/platform workers, 21, 25, 64
    income statement, 20–21
    mechanics, 23, 25
    P&D drivers, 21, 25, 64
weaknesses internal/external, 2
weight
    breaks, 69
    fundamentals of, 99
    highway, 59
    shipment, 50, 61–62, 65, 122, 126,
        126**t**
what-if scenarios, 100
worker's compensation, 21

Z
zip code, 52